Start

A story of life under a compulsory
community treatment order

GRAHAM MORGAN

Start
Graham Morgan

© Graham Morgan 2018

Published by:
Fledgling Press Ltd,
1 Milton Road West,
Edinburgh,
EH15 1LA

www.fledglingpress.co.uk

ISBN 9781912280070

Printed and bound by:
MBM Print SCS Ltd, Glasgow

MIX
Paper from
responsible sources
FSC® C117931

For Wendy McAuslan

Acknowledgements

I would like to thank Clare Cain from Fledgling Press as editor of this book. I have happy memories of sitting at my kitchen table typing away and nattering and that first excited, nervous meeting in the National Library of Scotland.

I would especially like to thank Andrew Greig for his support and advice over the long years of writing and Ailsa Crum for some well-timed advice that set me on the right direction. I would like to thank the writers who gathered in Achmelvich Hostel; I have fond memories of perching on my bunk bed, typing and wittering in the evening. The staff and tutors at Moniack Mhor were also incredibly helpful over the many weekends I stayed with them as part of my work with HUG.

I would also like to thank the many people who read different drafts of this book and gave feedback or encouragement including; Anita Murray, Mandy Haggith, Kate Ashton, Lesley Glaister, Jon King, Paulina Duncan, Frances Simpson, Marianne Morritt, Cynthia Rogerson, Helen Allison, Jules Wreford, Maggie Wallis, Donald Lyons, Phil Baardo, Angela Diaz, Mary Mowat, Be Morris, Lynn Doig, Gill Murray, Sheila Miller, Valerie MacBeath and Brendan McClusky.

I would like to thank my family for their patience and forbearance, especially Alan Morgan, Juliet Morgan, Keri Woods and Kathryn Morgan for their comments on the various drafts. Ffinlo Costain, Jon King and Cath King need a special mention for helping me work out how to approach publishers.

And finally, Wendy McAuslan needs thanks for inspiring me to write the book and for bringing me down to earth from my flights of fancy, and her children: Charlotte and James Golcher, for helping me realise that laughter and bouncing around the house are far more important than vague missions to change the world.

Some thoughts on START

Everyone with an interest in mental illness should read this book. It should prescribed reading for anyone caring for them, and essential for relatives and friends. Graham Morgan knows what he is talking about, and he conveys it with such lucidity, humility and love that you can't fail to get his message.

Absent from this book is any whiff of self-pity, bitterness or blame. It's hard to see how the author has arrived at this point in such a state of grace, given his experience at the hands of life in general and his fellow human beings in particular.

Graham Morgan is a prominent figure in his role as patient/client advocate on the 'mental health' scene both nationally and internationally. He is accustomed to addressing 'expert' audiences of eminent medical people and policy-makers. But this book speaks straight to the human heart.

In tracing his 'journey' from repeated crisis intervention to life back in the community under compulsory treatment, he offers us a rare glimpse of how it feels as a strong, sensitive young man to be judged, detained, and subjected to the constant strain of relative powerlessness within the 'caring relationship' with professionals.

Most profoundly, he teaches us what we do to those who diverge from the norms and mores of this particular corner of western society, those whose inner world we do not and will not understand and respect. About the loneliness we inflict upon them, the terrible privations of the outsider, vilified and controlled.

That the twenty-first-century finds us still here: with all our 'professionals', our medicine, psychology and psychiatry... it should make us weep blood.

Kate Ashton – *writer, former nurse and nursing journalist*

Graham Morgan's START is a remarkable and engrossing read. It buttonholed me and held my attention with its fervour, modesty, wit, self-questioning, its generosity amid corrosive fear, loss and pain. As a story through depression and psychosis and family dramas, I found it absorbing and funny, terrifying and celebratory. It is lyrical about love and being in the world, while being truly frightening. It's fresh and direct, unguarded and brave. It made me wince and chuckle.

Yes, it's a story about living with mental illness, but what I get from it is a sense of connection, that this is an extreme end of a spectrum we all to some extent live on, and as such it is profoundly moving and insightful.

It is humane, valuable, and in an important sense deeply sane.

Andrew Greig, *author of Electric Brae, That Summer, Fair Helen*

This is a moving, tender-hearted memoir that leads us, gently, into the shocking world of the mental health system. Graham Morgan is a consummate story teller, who shows us what it means to be brave, humane, funny and, above all, loving.

Mandy Haggith, *author of The Walrus Mutterer, Bear Witness and others*

-

START is a brave and generously candid book, embroidered in and singing the wee details that make life still beautiful and bearable, despite ourselves. It weaves many truths and fears I've never read or heard, but desperately wanted to hear expressed before, eloquently and intimately. The joy and despair; pleasure and longing that is staying alive. I cannot wait to share this book.

Laura Hird, *author of Born Free*

Graham Morgan speaks from the heart about the reality of mental illness. There is nothing sentimental or melodramatic or particularly consoling in START. He tells it like it is, with an eye to the unexpected beauty and humanity in everyday occurrences. I am so lucky, is a refrain echoing through many chapters. Highly readable, START is a refreshingly honest and warm, sometimes humorous, account of –not just his days, but life in general. I was moved by Morgan's sheer good natured generosity in the face of a debilitating life-shortening illness.

Cynthia Rogerson, *author of Love Letters from my Death-bed, I Love You, Goodbye, Stepping Out*

START took me by surprise. It is so gently and easily written – like listening to a conversation – but the simple words are infused with feelings that gradually reveal themselves – like the narrative itself – and they crept up on me – took me unawares. So I found myself unexpectedly moved to tears by simple descriptions of the people in Graham's life who love him – even though in fact he says very little about them.

This story is about as many different things as there are people who will read it. I have not lived with the nightmare of having a diagnosis of schizophrenia and so cannot possibly identify with that experience. But I identified with so much else that is in Graham's story: love, friendship, kindness, hugs and human contact. But what makes this such a powerful and complex story for me, is that Graham's struggle to understand his own identity and place in his world, is confined within this diagnosis that questions and challenges everything we think we know about truth and reality.

A wonderful story. Simply written, powerful in its emotional impact, exploring all the important things that connect us together, make us feel loved and secure, and help us to understand our place in the world.

Frances Simpson – *CEO Support in Mind Scotland*

A compelling read, from the beautiful prose, the wonder of the natural world to the depths of despond of living with schizophrenia. The roller coaster of a life laid out on the page for all of us to learn from will enhance any family members, friend or professionals understanding of the journey people take through mental illness.

Ruth Stark *MSc, CQSW, MBE – Immediate Past President, International Federation of Social Work*

-

Beautifully written! Graham took me on an intensely personal journey to old familiar places, mental and physical, giving me a whole new perspective on so many of them.

Graham's knowledge, life experience and expertise leap off every page. He fearlessly looks at many of the issues in the world of mental ill health – recognising that we, as campaigners, aren't a homogeneous group – and what a wonderful thing that is! Thanks to his wonderfully engaging writing style, I feel like I've come to know myself a little better.

Chris Young – *author of Tales of a Wandering Loon.*

LIFE AT THE LINKS CAFE

I blame my medication for my weight.

When I am giving lectures, I say that before I went on to Olanzapine I weighed 10 stone and that now I weigh 16 stone.

I make jokes and say the NHS should give us a clothing allowance when it makes us take drugs that pile on the weight and then I get a wee bit more serious and talk of diabetes.

Sometimes I get even more serious and say that people with my diagnosis die twenty years earlier than the rest of the population and then I do that wry laugh and say my age and that I must be living on borrowed time by now.

When I get home, I think of the promises I have made to walk the beach and the forest in the evening and the early morning. I think of my sister-in-law making me commit to climbing a Munro on my fiftieth birthday. I somehow doubt I will.

Usually I sit down heavily on the couch, I pour a whisky and keep on pouring so that if I am asked, I can say that I only drank two whiskies last night, or I save the whisky for later so that it doesn't look like I have drunk two bottles this week and I pour a huge tumbler of martini and gin, trying to convince myself that it is more healthy than you would think because of the vermouth.

And slowly, as I slip into a haze, I think to myself that I know that these drugs put on weight, I know what chips and mayonnaise do. I know what walking from the car to the office and the office to the car does, and what drinking does and having two sugars in my coffee and not sleeping.

I know what I should be doing but, in the haze, as I watch *How I Met Your Mother*, I think to myself that it's been a busy day. That tomorrow I will walk, then the next day I will swim, that tonight I will take a drink to bed with me but not the next night.

*

When I think how many people with a severe mental illness have not even touched another person in the last year, I feel like weeping. I think of the overpowering loneliness, that gripping pain of the clenched throat of misery that says, 'Someone, someone, speak to me, listen to me. Someone smile at me as if you wanted to smile at me without me wondering how much you are paid an hour to do that.

When I think of this, I pause and think to myself that I am very, very, lucky indeed. I think of the people that I meet in the café. The Links Café which has almost become an institution in our lives. I think of when I am sitting uncomfortably on the seats in mid-summer, the seats on the bench table just out of the wind, in the corner the café makes with the open air swimming pool.

It glares an awesome blueness and is surrounded by iron railings. The dogs are tied up there while we drink coffee. They sit almost patiently. Sometimes Benson will climb over another dog and get tangled up in his lead, or the collie dogs will suddenly bare their sharp teeth at another dog. Maybe Benson will lie down on his back and Taffy will grip his throat between her teeth but both will have wagging tails. On occasion, when they are tied near the sandpit that they have dug in the corner over the years, they will lie down, their heads poking over the rim.

Then, while they lie there, while we talk, Cara will totter up to them with the water bottle that seems bigger than her, to fill up their drinking bowls and they will drink and then knock the bowls over, and Cara will refill them over and over until, on hot days, she empties the bottle over their heads and bursts out laughing at their expressions.

All the adults will be talking: about dogs, children, husbands, school, work and the week ahead; whether Jean will come by before we all go away and I will be sitting a wee bit to the side.

When I am at the table, I always struggle with the empty sugar packets; you screw them up but there is nowhere to put them, so I twist them very small and by and by they will flick away in the wind to become the litter I pretend to have nothing to do with.

I say very little at the café. I tend to smile and give Cara packets of sauce to play with. I sometimes think of buying toast but I am trying to budget so I don't.

I sit there basking; feeling uncomfortably happy, my bag and coat on the ground. That is often commented on because it is so untidy.

After a time, Sally will go off to the park or the beach to play with Gavin. Or if she doesn't do that, she will ask to go to the other park and Cara will ask if she can go to the park too and Sarah will say 'Not just yet,' because everyone is busy. Then I will offer to take her with me.

Delighted at the gratitude Sarah gives me, even more delighted at the feel of Cara's tiny hand in mine as she balances along the swimming pool wall, pausing to hold out both hands for me to hold while she jumps off.

We will spend the next half hour or so in the park. I will trail after her, swing her on the baby swing, till suddenly she says,

'Stop!'

We will pause by the grate at the entrance to the pool and push pebbles and grass she has collected through the gaps.

She will climb the stairs to the slide, grumbling that she has to hold my hand. Then she will insist that I sit at the bottom so that when she reaches the end of the slide, she can be caught.

On a couple of occasions she has toppled off. She just leans sideways in slow motion and falls to the rubberised floor; then I will rush and hold her to me until she stops crying. After that we may go to the pirate ship to peek out of the plastic windows or for her to leap into my arms from the deck.

At other times when no one else is on the roundabout, she will make me lie on my back and stare at the sky while she wheels it round and round. Sometimes the circling of the roundabout overtakes her and she falls over but at other times she climbs on, lies down beside me and we both stare into the blue and the clouds as the roundabout goes round and round, more and more slowly.

After that we go back to the adults at the café. And Gladys and Hamish will go away to the cinema or to the shops, and Kay and me and Sarah will walk on the beach with the dogs and the children. The two dogs go wild, rushing through the shallows, biting each other, running shoulder to shoulder chasing sticks. I tend to wheel Cara in her buggy while Sarah and Kay talk and Sally will be away doing small girl beach things.

Sometimes Cara will remember I am pushing the buggy and cry out for her mummy to push it. At other times Cara will walk along the beach, collecting stones to put in the water or to carry up the beach to place in the buggy. And these are the very best times.

Walking, pushing the pram, talking; the dog always getting into trouble; strangers stopping us and assuming we are a couple, which makes me glow because I would like to be a dad again and a couple again with someone, one day.

At the gate to her house Sarah will pause before getting lunch and going out to the supermarket for food and nappies; getting ready for the rest of the weekend with her boyfriend, and I will say goodbye and set off for home.

I will pass the old man with the crossed kukris carved into his wall. He will be smoking his cigarette; the one-eyed dog will be sniffing through the mesh of the fence and for a time we will talk. Never about much. I always wonder how he knows my name. I always feel embarrassed that I don't know his. I often think to myself.

'Wow, he is even lonelier than me!'

And it is always me who leaves; me, who pretends to be busy as I go back to my flat and the mattress on the floor and the pile of whisky bottles in the wee cupboard under the stairs where the cooker is and the tiny sink.

I could paint that picture, the one of me being lonely and it would be true and yet it isn't. There are a hundred million versions of me and none of them are true and none of them are false. It is just that at some times some of the pictures are more true to me, and maybe to you, than at other times.

When everyone is busy on a Saturday and I am in town, wandering in and out of the charity shops, I am occasionally very, very happy. I feel that delighted recognition when I find a book of Scottish literature, maybe James Roberston or Andrew Greig or Alan Bisset, once Kevin McNeil.

For a time it became a regular occurrence to find just the books I would have liked to buy but couldn't afford. I wondered who it was in Nairn who read the same books as me and put them by for the charity shops. At other times, because I was alone, I would find that awkward thrill of picking up romances by Jodi Picoult and Freya North, delighting myself with evenings curled up on the couch reading stories where there are always good endings and those tender kisses I miss so much. Those exciting times when emotion runs high and mini adventures scatter themselves all over the page.

Much as I would like to, I cannot persuade myself that fifty-two hours a year peering at secondhand books in charity shops is an adventure. For me, my big adventure when I moved here was when I started buying clothes in the charity shops. Initially I had relied on people like Jean or my sister-in-law to help me with clothes. I just don't have the sense of what is a good cloth and what isn't.

I don't know what my measurements are. I don't know how clothes are meant to hang or fit or look or feel. But lately, I no longer feel that anxiety that stops me riffling through the hangers. I grab at the clothes and plonk myself in the changing room, almost always regretting wearing shoes with too many lace holes.

I now have a growing collection of beige trousers and shirts that almost fills the cloth-framed wardrobe I bought in Aldi last year.

And then I go home. Often I pop into the organic vegan deli where the owners know me vaguely and sometimes I pop into the fruit and veg shop which smells so rich; that has piles of glistening tomatoes and stacks of glowing oranges and bundles of herbs. They are far too expensive.

It makes me think what my wife would think if she saw me buying value tomatoes and mushrooms past their sell-by date when not so long ago our weekly shop was always Fairtrade, always organic.

And I buy the *Guardian*. Every week I buy the *Guardian* on Saturday. I sit at home in my flat, in my untidy flat, and there I read about recipes for meals with pomegranate syrup and sumac, for marsh samphire and sea bass and I read the indignant articles about everything we all have to get indignant about.

I get a wee bit tired of being so predictably angry about everything, sometimes I catch sight of the heresy people feel about me when I say, the Israelis need somewhere to live too, the ineptitude with which I wonder if nuclear power is better than oil. Generally, though, I eat up the little injustices; store up my passion for this and that, the issues I am meant to be passionate about.

Mainly I read about that man in a band in the magazine who makes fun of his wife and children and dog every week; who makes fun of them so much that you know he loves them more than he knows how to hold his love.

I like him. I could never talk to him but I would like to nod at him in the park when I walk the dog I don't have. I like the photographs. I like the blind date page and imagine doing it myself. I love it when they have a great time together.

I look at the varied aged models with approval but still look to see which is the prettiest. The one I would like to walk along the beach holding hands with.

And then it is time to cook tea, take out the whisky and watch telly, to get that wee bit muzzy, a wee bit glaikit, a wee bit sad before going to bed and falling asleep with the light and the radio on.

To wake and fumble for the light switch, to turn off the radio again and find my thoughts catching me up in the darkness; bundles of anxiety slipping round the corners of my mind, setting off alarms and;

'What ifs' and; 'Why did she say that?' and; 'How will I do that?'

And at times I deliberately make my jaw soft, make my forehead smooth and say, 'Let those thoughts drift away, drift away like dandelion clocks. Let your anxiety fade from your mind and the quiet oasis of sleep take you away.'

For a few seconds I find myself in limbo until, with a roar, the anxiety and the thinking rushes back in. *Those dandelions have been flung into a rainstorm of cumulonimbus. They are flying all over the place, getting drenched by the heavy raindrops*, and I am thinking, thinking, thinking and I don't know what I am thinking but it is battering me. I hate the screech of my thoughts.

I turn the radio back on and it fades to a murmur that I do not notice, the world is an absence and I am not there anymore. I am gone. I am at peace.

In the morning I will wake to the tangled sheets. I will feel joy that I can lie still and do nothing, feel nothing, conscious just of the sensation of my toes at the end of the bedclothes and the downie still wrapped round my head. Conscious that at some point it will be time to sit on the couch drinking coffee and, because it is a Sunday, having toast and an egg at the bare table in the corner of the living room.

January

LOVE IN A MODERN CLIMATE

I live by the sound of beeping texts. I begin to breathe at the sound of a voice that I am only just beginning to know. I begin to break the bonds of a long, long isolation.

I talk to you through the night; as I go to bed I shine and natter in silence. I am so keen to share my words that I forget to sleep. I am so keen to learn about you that I wake up, become alert as the night goes quiet and the sound of cars in the street becomes a lonely hiss.

I talk to you in the morning and on the bus. I talk to you at work; I give you a great big hug in the middle of an important meeting.

I slip my awareness into the tapping of my fingers upon your waiting body. I wake up, I untangle my chains, I snap out the keys and type a message of liberation and in a brief instant I am free of the weight of the long gone, cold and heavy past.

I learn to sleep again, I learn not to yearn and I learn to yearn all over again. I kiss your fingers and hear the beep, beep of your reply.

The locks are non-existent. I have made them vanish, to fall and rust in a heap amongst the stinging nettles.

DOORSTEP SALESMAN

I suppose I have left you a wee bit confused. I've walked up to you and started talking. Busy talking of this and that and what I think and do and you don't know me.

I'm a stranger in the street, a drunkard at a party, a politician shaking your hand when you have answered the door, all bleary-eyed in the late morning.

I do want to speak to you and I do want you to listen to me and somehow I need to convince you there is some merit, some point in reading these pages.

Now, I am not well known, I am not a celebrity and I am not some hyper-successful or clever person and I am not even a journalist or an academic. I am neither the salt of the earth nor a businessman. I am nothing much really.

I am just someone saying hello; I have walked through the door and I am nervous but I would like to introduce myself to you. I would like to be brave enough to shake your hand or give you a hug and to say:

'Let us sit down and share a coffee or a whisky and let me tell you who I am and what I do.'

I'm an ex-public schoolboy who didn't join any old boys' network. I'm a failed university student who failed his exams on purpose to prove he didn't care that he was going to fail anyway. I am the son of two lovely people but took years to know their loveliness, or what about, I am the brother of an amazing sister and brother, but somehow forgot to speak to them? I am an Englishman who moved up to Scotland to live with his love and who has now lived in Scotland for longer than ever he lived in England. No, forget that. I am someone who walked out on his wife and his son and life was never the same again. No, not that. I am an activist and a leader in an obscure world of social justice and mental health. Well, not really. A leader? Me? Watch me networking: I scuff my shoes and stare at the floor and answer in monosyllables. I am a lonely man who became old without noticing. I yearn for romance but know that will not happen; that my tiny home and my untidy bed are where I will stay for ever, till my eyes go rheumy and my hands shake and I get frightened when I climb out of my chair at the end of the evening.

I am the son of a squadron leader, an ocean racer, a yacht builder and yacht seller. A larger-than-life man, a man of appetite and opinion that could lead him to trouble in anything from ordering food in a restaurant, to keeping relationships and having the right sort of relationships, to managing the staff in his business and who, now I know him better, I love very much indeed. I am the son of a mother who mothered and sold yacht charters and once was a nurse and who has volunteered for the Samaritans for decades and decades; who has friends everywhere; who is someone to confide in and reach peaks of silliness with when cooking together, and both of whom are so much more than these descriptions provide.

I have a younger brother who is the deputy medical director of a mental health trust in England and who skis in far off mountains, cycles miles along country roads, runs whenever he can and cooks, just like me, to prove he loves people, and who has a lovely wife and amazing children that I am just learning to talk to.

I am also the elder brother to my sister who lives in Glastonbury and who likes to make fun of all the Glastonbury types and yet is really one herself. She is soon to qualify as a midwife and has spent years as a doula, not that I really know what one is. She loves adventures in the wilds, walks with women of all sorts. She loves swimming in cold lakes and camping in remote clearings and has a thriving family of lots of children and a lovely partner.

My dad is the son of a Welshman who was an insurance salesman, served in the army in the war in India and was once a fish and chip shop owner in London, and somehow connected to the silver-tongued preacher of the Rhonda Valleys. He was part of a family that sold tea and lived in a big, big house. I remember him for the sixpences he pulled out of the air; his car that had seats wrapped in the original protective packaging and his prayers. My dad is the son of a mother who was a London Welshwoman; who fretted for his health and was as staunch a Methodist (or is it Baptist?) as her husband was. She made good cakes and kept the garden well. I remember her for her smell, for sweets and cups of tea in bed with the radio on in the morning; for the fact that there was a stash of those ancient huge, white, five pound notes left hidden in the house when she died.

And my mum. She was the daughter of a man who did lots of jobs; cleaning boilers of asbestos, sailing in the merchant navy in the Arctic convoys in WWII, and running a hotel in Teignmouth with his wife, which got flooded and wasn't insured and so they lost it. They got divorced when my mum was young which was a big thing in those days, especially as my mum was a pupil in the local convent at the time, with her sister. My main memories of him involve him taking us to a loganberry patch, swimming in the sea in winter and shaving with a cut throat razor.

Her mother did lots of odd jobs too; mainly being a lady's companion in different parts of the country. I remember her for so much; for always mixing me and my brother up; for her giggle and her sherry; for her hip joints that you could hear rubbing as she walked and for her caustic opinions about almost everything. My memory is that she was some sort of right wing socialist if that illogicality is possible; my brother's memory is that she was a mad old coot, but she was a great woman to know. She walked even more than my mum does and lived for so long that she began to say that she had lived longer than she wanted to; that she was weary of being alive.

They all have fascinating stories that I can never remember; somehow or other we have a connection to the Island of St Helena and also perhaps to Portugal. Isn't that amazing? Isn't everyone's story amazing?

I have an MBE for services to mental health but I'm not really sure why. I have a wee plastic statue which was an award from the Royal College of Psychiatrists. I was a member of the Millan Committee that did the work for the current Scottish Mental Health (2003) Care and Treatment Act. (That's the one I am now detained under).

My work is about rights and conversations and changing the world for people like me. I enjoy it; I like meeting people and sharing ideas and learning from each other. I like writing reports and speeches and articles and turning up at meetings and helping people speak out.

I am surrounded by lots of people, lots of wonderful people and, between us, we witter and sometimes this wittering does indeed create change; which usually surprises me.

I'm just coming up to the end of my fifth year of my current community detention. I think my story will finish when it is either renewed or stopped at my tribunal after the New Year.

I wonder who you are? Who you are and what we could talk about? I want to sit down on a bench and learn how to talk to you.

WALKING TOGETHER: OUT OF RHYTHM

Besides the edge of the road the water has crept up, the grass and the reeds poke out, making reflections in the setting sun on the still water.

I wonder what the fishes think; swimming over what was once the edge of their world, whether they might be frightened or a bit bemused or maybe they are just fish-like, being fishes, swimming looking for something to munch on.

Away in the sky a heron flaps; they always look so heavy and weary and ungainly and yet somehow special and wonderful.

The crows are flying home and the sun is sending streaks out from beneath the clouds. There is no smell of woodsmoke though there should be, there is not even a hint of mist rising from the water though there should be.

Everything is still and is quiet.

I stand at the edge of the water, a slight ridge of water round the soles of my shoes. The driftwood and the driftweed and the driftstraw is tangled in shapes made by the flow of the water and I think I should take a picture of it. Remember it.

My cheeks feel cold. A couple of ducks fly noisily overhead.

It is the end of my New Year's holidays. Tomorrow my mind will light up like a neon sign and I will start buzzing and carry on buzzing for months until I find those brief few weeks to stop and to slow and to become still and warm and vague-eyed and sleepy-headed and just so, so, gentle to the day. My mind and all that work energy will become a reassuring hum and the passion a reasonable commitment and the anxiety a distant murmur.

And I will turn round and hold your hand and lean my head against your head and slip my arm around your waist. We will brush our lips together and then we will smile and say together that being still and boring is the most amazing, exciting, wonderful, passionate thing we can ever do and we will amble away from the shore, remarking about how out of rhythm our steps are, mumbling about nothing much and glowing, making people avert their eyes from our soppy smiles.

MY UNIVERSE

My universe, for so many years, was my wife and my son. We were a tight spiral which threw out the outside world; other people were an occasional encounter, an almost afterthought. I based my thinking on what they thought and who they were. I lived on the edge of always wanting to please and nervous of that very pleasing, drifting beside the world they created for us.

They were there in the morning and the evening, and between us we worked out what we would eat and how we would clothe ourselves. I thought they were the only people that I was truly bound to, the only people that made up my vision of me and them and the world around us.

And yet. And yet somehow, over a number of years that universe lost its definition and its boundaries. Those things that seemed certain lost their solidity and the things that I had hoped for and dreamed about became pale and less certain.

I had always worked and worked. I knew little other than the need to work and to do all that changing the world stuff, and at work I had a different world and met different people. Over time the attractions of that world grew on me and the attractions of the people in that world grew on me. In particular, Sarah, who I worked with. She was pretty and passionate and wonderfully good at listening to the anxieties and disappointments I experienced over those years I spent with my wife. And I was wonderfully good at confiding in her.

We never had an affair, we did not even hug very much and never went anywhere approaching a kiss, but I found I became a listening ear to her different stories of her own awkward relationship and she, my haven, to talk about the difficulties in mine. And so, our hearts became a bit tangled, a bit confused, which served no good purpose when I tried to sort the problems I was having in my marriage. Which, in fact, hastened its destruction. Somehow, all along, that friendship which had seemed the perfect place, the only place to share the increasing misery of a marriage that had slowly been going wrong, that place where I was admired and free to express myself became its own poisonous and yet wonderfully attractive harbour from sadness.

Those years of destruction were so, so, difficult and the way my marriage suddenly dissolved, so unexpected. I still do not believe that I had the courage to walk out, or for that matter, the cruelty.

Since then my life has felt increasingly bizarre. I do not understand it at all; my universe is now a tiny flat and a life I do not quite grasp. On one level I am meeting people; I am daring to go out to parties and out for walks. I will cook friends meals; I will stay over at people's houses, I will walk across muddy fields and be given confidences and stories that I would never have expected before and this makes me feel valued and treasured.

I go camping with friends and look after wee children. I go on trips for no particular reason other than the fun of it. I have started speaking to my brother and sister and my parents properly. For the first time in decades, I can do what I want, when I want and how I want.

If I feel like eating pizza with so much cheese on it, it melts and slithers off onto the plate. If I want to drink whisky at two in the morning or walk to the harbour at five in the morning. If I want to talk to myself or stride the weekend away. If I want to work late and early and all the hours in between, I can do. If I want to be miserable, if I want to skulk and stare at nothing, if I want to write long verses of different sorts of agony, I can do.

I hadn't a clue. In my naivety and cruelty, I thought that leaving my wife would mean that I would live a short drive away from her, that I would be free; that I would be free to do the things I wanted to do and to think the things I wanted to think, but I still thought I would see her. I thought I would visit frequently and that after the initial upset, we would be friends again. In fact, much better friends than when we were married. I thought I would be part of my son's growing up, that I would watch over him as he went to university and share ideas with his mum on how to make his life as good and as free of problems as it could be, and that maybe we would become close in a new, different but maybe very positive way.

It wasn't like that, it wasn't like that at all. I do not ever speak to my wife, or rather, she has made it clear she does not want to speak to me. I do not hear from my son, I do not speak to more than a couple of our friends from all those decades of marriage.

Instead, my admissions to hospital continue and that ache of loneliness, that jolt of insecurity and that fear of newness and change oppresses me and I find myself not even marching down a lonely road but shuffling into sleepless nights and evenings made bleary with alcohol. I do the friends bit and the new life bit and it is exciting in its way but still I dread the night-times; those times when listening to radio shows about third world football matches, early in the morning on the World Service, is a welcome distraction from the thoughts I surround myself with every day and every moment and, those thoughts, I hate them so.

February

FINDING ST PETER AND ITS ASBESTOS

It is wonderful visiting these ruins but then everything seems wonderful nowadays. I suppose I must get a bit boring about the wonderful things, a return to the preening and saying 'look at us lucky happy people!' The sort of self-congratulation that makes people loathe newsletters at Christmas.

Of course, it is not always like that. The arrival of love does not somehow magic that darkness away, does not make the uncertainty disappear. Sometimes I think it enhances it, makes it worse. I remember my sister-in-law saying how surprising it was that Wendy fell for me, or maybe how attractive and fun she was and that I was lucky indeed. And I must admit that I find it hard to believe: a schizophrenic, overweight, unfit, almost alcoholic who spends the majority of his life in silence is really not the most desirable option. Especially as I keep getting things wrong. Wendy often catches me trying to buy the very worst of clothing; trousers that end above my ankles, shirts that bulge over my stomach revealing just how fat I am getting. Then she has to listen to music that just doesn't work: my iPod shifts from Frank Sinatra to Beethoven's Choral to Nirvana to Beyoncé without a pause. We can just be settling down to tea with Rihanna singing away and have a sudden switch to Armenian folk music followed by the *Symphony of Sorrowful Songs*; it really doesn't work.

She also claims that I am one of only two people that she has met in her life who cannot tell what rhythm or a beat is. She shakes her head in bemusement when I tap along to music without any reference at all as to how it should go. And then, lo and behold, my buried stories. When I first met Wendy she was so adamant that she really did not like the sort of macho-type, the sort of adventure stories some men have. And yet they are really my last reserve: ones that I dredge up when I revisit my twenties; tales of walking in minefields in Israel, dodging cargo ships that were trying to rescue us, much against our will, in the mid-Atlantic, finding a hollow island in the Philippines and in the neighbouring island, a cave with skeletons strewn all over a cave floor, sailing with tornadoes around us in the Irish sea, climbing cliffs and having grown men spend the afternoon admiring my agility and technique when I was not quite an adolescent.

I keep those stories in reserve, hoping that they will challenge people's preconceptions of me but Wendy is not only not impressed, I think she would have a name for people who show off in that way.

Oh, I really, really do not know what she sees in me. Even my cooking can horrify her; the liberal use of oil and spices and strange Middle Eastern and Asian ingredients. I remember the Korean meal that I slaved over; she said the noodles were just like worms and wouldn't eat the stuffed tofu at all.

I live with the fear that she will come to her senses and realise that her choice has really been a very unwise one, that she should go back to the husband she left some time ago or find some urbane, solvent, funny someone-or-other.

And yet she does love me. I am too modest to mention the compliments she gives me, but they make me so unutterably pleased with myself, so convinced she sees something in me that in my wildest dreams I could not access.

We do share things that we enjoy; lately we have been taking journeys to visit abandoned buildings which is amazing. We started some time ago with St Peter's Seminary before they began doing it up, skipping past the asbestos signs and the dirty syringes, fascinated and frightened of it at the same time, amazed by all the graffiti and the sheer size of it, all hidden mouldering in the woods. After that it was Buchanan Castle at Drymen, where we met an American castle professor, imagine that! A professor who goes on field trips to visit ruined castles that you are forbidden to enter. He told us all about it and showed us the best way in past the barbed wire. It really is a fairytale ruin; it looks just like a ruined castle should, with its turrets and its ivy and its thicket of bamboo, and inside it really does have trees growing in the abandoned halls. I am glad we are both a bit scared of the world as we did have the sense that bits of it were likely to fall on us at any moment and so refrained from too much climbing around. And, lastly, we have just been to the abandoned village at Portavadie near the ferry crossing to Bute. A very surreal experience of eating a scrummy lunch at the spick and span marina followed by clambers among the musty houses of the village that was never lived in and which have been covered in huge murals.

I don't know what we like about it; walking into a ruin, a deserted mouldering place, hand in hand, expecting to be thrown out at any moment, sharing kisses in rooms with nettles and ferns growing amongst the floorboards, imagining what life would have been like. Finding sudden images that startle us, amuse us, astonish us and then creeping away, wishing we did things like that: camped among ruins, drawing pictures, making art and eating at bonfires amongst the deserted homes.

It doesn't matter, it is our current passion; find us an abandoned building and we will search it out, all excited like wee children about to be given a very special treat. A good thing for winter, for the season when it feels better to be indoors locked away from the gales and the rain. For the season when we wrap ourselves in each other and I can forget about that batting above my weight thing.

THE END OF THE WORLD

I have been sectioned lots of times in the past. That is, detained, made to take the treatment that is given me, kept from the sky and the fresh air and the freedom most of my friends do not question.

I am now under a compulsory community treatment order. I understand the reasoning in many ways; most people live in such a world that they cannot believe that evil is anything other than entertainment in a horror film. But I am evil of a different magnitude. If I could summon an ounce of integrity I would rid the world of something like me, and yet I don't. I relish the company of my friends, the luxury of my bed, the commitment of my work. I relish it so much that I ignore, as best I can, what I really am.

Most people seeing someone like me would say, 'This does not make sense. We must keep him from his darker thoughts, his incredible solutions. We must keep him safe.'

If they knew what I was really like they would not hesitate to do the opposite.

When my psychiatrist renews my section, he says that I literally believe that the evil lives in me, lives in me down my spine in a black slime, like the innards of a rotten tree trunk, and I am too polite to tell him that I'm not completely sure I believe that anymore. I know I did and when I am reminded, I can picture it, can see the devil resting there. I can think that if I cut myself open I would find that rot but I am not so sure of it anymore. A part of me sometimes thinks there might be nothing.

When I think nothing would be there, when I am in a room with my CPN or psychologist and we get talking of the evil, I can feel it rising in me, washing out in waves of malevolence and I want to suck it back in. I want to protect these nice people from me.

I cannot see it but if I could, it would be a black cloud of tiny rays of energy seeping into people's skin like radiation, sucking away that positivity, that face that tilts to the sun with joy, those arms that cuddle a lover and those hands that feed a baby, write a letter, gather the toys into a corner before picking up the phone to chat the night away.

I do not understand why I live in contradictions. I do not understand how at one moment I can say I am an atheist and the next say that I believe in devils and the end of the world. I do not understand how I can live a life that is built on contradiction. I do not understand how I can know something to be true and yet be completely incapable of sustaining that argument when challenged, or at least explaining the discrepancies of my existence.

That the world is a balance of good and bad and without the bad the good couldn't do what the good does.

I get angry that I am bad because I want to be good. I would have liked to be an angel making people giggle and dance.

Instead I move amongst people, seeming to be gentle and charming and all the while sucking the energy from the world, all the time turning the positivity into the blankness of despair and grief.

No one knows I do it. No one ever believes me.

When I am being 'therapized' or sitting on the hospital bed, they ask me to tell them about the evil I have done. Just a few examples so that they can understand and I tell them that is not the point. Being bad and wicked like a murderer or an abuser, like a Hitler or a Stalin is not the point. That is not evil, not the evil that leaches the universe's energy away, turns light into darkness.

I say, 'Do you not get it? I am that essence. I do not do wicked things. I summon the darkness around you and for that there should be no forgiveness.'

At these times, when I let myself think this, I seize on those people who say it is such an arrogant thing to believe you are so important. I dare that hope that says maybe it is all some big, big mistake.

Maybe I invent cloud castles, maybe this fear of what I am is a silly wee game I got lost in. Maybe the medication is good, is helpful. Maybe, as they say, it gives me the almost high-achieving, high-powered life I never would have had without it.

At other times I find the night and the dark future forbidding. I think to myself that one day I will have to face up to my badness, get rid of it, cut it all away and then, when I am feeling this rip of disgust, when I am wandering round the house saying, 'I want to die,' I think of the geese flying overhead in autumn and of the early dawn in summer. I think so hard of the wonderful, wonderful world I inhabit and I shiver and try to avoid all thought of my likely destiny.

Ah! What a story I tell. There you are, sitting down for a pleasant read and here I am busy talking of the sadness and the terror of what people call mental illness.

When I say 'What people call mental illness', I have to qualify myself, explain.

I know we can contemplate the existence of different realities. I know we can deny that this state exists, that it may be a construct of the drug companies, a way of society controlling us, a way of isolating difference and making it other, in the sense of 'wrong', a way of medicalising ordinary existence.

That it can be a human response to trauma and the anguish of the lives we lead but I don't really care.

I know the mind can go wrong, that the brain can go wrong, and I do not really care what it is that makes it go wrong. I do not understand those people who plead for trauma to be the cause, as though that makes it all better, as though that would stop them from feeling guilty. As though that is something they can fix and alter and that somehow the use of words and the manipulation of feelings is somehow more ethical than the use of medication or the administering of a whole variety of different treatments.

Sometimes, I must admit, I am tempted to say,

'But who decides what illness is?'

Why is one way of behaving and thinking seen as illness and the other not so? Just as people with autism are now seen as 'neuro-atypical' compared to the 'normal' 'neuro-typical' people, so could people with a mental illness be seen as atypical to something or other, and could we not accept this difference, cherish it even?

But then I sit down and think to myself about all the many, many people I know and I think,

I am not interested.

I do not want to celebrate this form of difference. I do not want to say we should be proud of the way we are – wear the 'Glad to be mad' t-shirt or dance the 'Largactil shuffle' in a burst of excited rebellion.

No. To me, when my friends are glazed with sadness, so glazed and consumed that they cannot muster the energy to step foot outside the door, so lacking in confidence that they are unable to take the decision to make a cup of tea, then I think,

This is horrific.

When my companions talk of rays coming from the television that are being beamed from the Ministry of Defence, and when they are busy tearing up each gesture of love and trust in a desperate attempt to show themselves how unlovable they are, when all they crave is a cuddle. Then I think,

This is unacceptable.

When I see my friends and they are filled with an everlasting anger and an undimmed capacity for argument I think,

Give them some sleep, some peace.

When I remember the long, long roll call of the people I have known, in fact, a roll call that is so long I no longer have the confidence to get it right when I list it in my head. That roll call of people who have loathed themselves and the world so much, who have been in such unbearable, almost unimaginable pain that they have jumped off cliffs, hung themselves from trees, swum out to sea, swallowed pills, walked in front of trains, fallen off bridges, I think to myself,

Why are we so suspicious of medication? Why are we not ploughing billions into pills, into research, into the jar that contains happiness, the shock that brings peace, the magic words that create calm. Absolutely anything that may stop this and maybe those billions could somehow promote that jagged exhale that says,

33

'At last I can stop.'

and I say:

'I don't care anymore.'

I don't know how this can be achieved, I don't care what the latest brainchild brainwave will do. I know with all my heart that the peace we crave is an illusion, but let us find routes out of the arguments and ideologies into those small gifts that say,

'I am loved, I am soft. I am allowed, occasionally, to be happy.'

The story goes on and on, fashioning itself like a conversation at a party you want to escape from. Because mainly I am happy. I am glad to be where I am, I am full of the joy of being me. I'm Graham, being me.

A happy, happy, lonely Graham.

CELEBRATIONS

That moment when I walk into the room with Wendy. My whole family are there, all smiling, laughing, shouting out,

'Happy birthday!'

And that is Wendy's introduction to everyone. In one moment my brother and sister, my mum and dad and nephews and nieces are just half-remembered names, slight echoes of the stories I have told her. And then, the next moment, after travelling for ages on the train up to Pitlochry and then sharing a cosy car ride to the farmhouse and its hostel above Loch Tay, she walks through a door and is in the midst of 13 brand new family members; everyone except my son.

I abandon her for a glass of wine while she whirls round a succession of kisses and hugs and introductions, to cuddle up to me later and say,

'Graham, never do that to me again!'

It is a lovely, lovely time. The whole hostel to ourselves in mid winter. The puddles crazed with ice, the steam rising off the cold loch, the hills pinky-red with their caps of snow outlined by the setting sun.

We take turns to cook. On John's night, he spends ages making different lasagnas, but on taking one huge dish from the oven the heat burns him, making him slop some of the bubbling cheese and meat over his hand and in turn drop most of it on the floor.

After a slight pause, my mum says, 'Oh dear! I'm sure we can rescue most of it.'

And one of the children giggles, at which point John shouts at us all to leave the room.

Down in the sitting room, waiting to open the fizzy wine, we stare at the floor but rapidly start grinning, very much naughty children caught doing the wrong thing but giggling none the less.

John comes down not much later and everyone makes speeches. I do like it: being told lovely things about me, being celebrated, being right in the middle of a loving group of people.

A weekend of walks through forests and up snowy paths, a weekend of jokes over chips in pubs, chocolate shops, walks by frozen waterfalls with hats and gloves and steamy breath. A weekend of crannogs and too much Bombay Sapphire. Of Wendy and me walking into the house after an outing; not noticing that my dad has not followed us in. Only much later do we find him, having eventually struggled out of the ditch by the house, into which he had fallen while we were mid conversation, so busy talking we did not notice he was no longer there.

I do like this, this melding, this gathering, these chances for laughter.

BETRAYAL

When I left my wife I did not know what would happen. It was a drama; a horrible, awful, bitter drama that ripped and tore and sapped our strength and made the world a place of slashed darkness where even sleep was frightening and tiring.

I had tried to leave once before. On another day of arguments and bitterness, it became something I could no longer stand. It had been building up and up and up and although we had spent months trying to be nice to each other, my niceness was a glaze. I had changed; I no longer wanted to send loving texts but I did.

I did not enjoy our conversation. I had given up on the hope of intimacy and did not want to rediscover it. I dreaded the thought of a life together. I dreaded the thought of trying to love when I no longer loved.

The effort my wife made was strong but fragile: a delicate attempt to change things but too late. I had grown separate and distant in my heart. Her attempts to reach it may have been met with a smile but my smile didn't convince me.

I can't quite remember the day I left. My friend Sarah, with whom I shared confidences and feelings that I shouldn't, had a baby, a wee girl, and sitting in the sitting room, my wife asked if I intended to visit them in the hospital and I said,

'Yes.'

And she told me that if I visited, that our relationship would be over and I said,

'Fine.'

And went to bed.

In the night she packed me some clothes and some of my possessions and in the morning I packed them into the car and left to stay at a friend's. Or it was something like that. I really don't know.

I remember, a few days later, being asked to speak to her by my seventeen-year-old son who said she was in a terrible state. We met on the shore by the sand dunes and she wept and she screamed and said she would die and that there would be no one to look after our son and that she couldn't stay in the house a moment longer. And she collapsed on the sand dunes and would not move and our son, who had been watching, walked away. And after a time I said to her that whatever she did I would not come back to her but she lay there and made no answer.

In the car my son was silent and would not talk and I said that I would take him home and give him what money I had, and if she didn't return I would try to sort something out. I left him at the house and turned round to go back to Nairn, where I had promised to meet Sarah to help her when her ex-partner came round to see his baby.

Halfway back on the Dava moor, I met my wife driving the other way; she stopped in the middle of the road but I swerved around her and then she chased me to Nairn.

It was a silly time and I feel silly emotions. I feel that sense that I am saying things I shouldn't say and yet I do not know why I cannot tell my story. I feel weary. I feel weary remembering. I feel weary about the commotion at Sarah's house where my wife had followed me anyway, and at her collapse and her tears and our drive into the middle of nowhere to talk, when I knew with every part of me that it was over. And I feel weary about the memory of going back to the house to stay because she said she would die if I didn't and that she couldn't look after our son anymore.

I feel weary that my son would not speak with me or eat in the same room. That he decided to sleep in my room and that I should sleep in his room, that he did not want me in the house and so two weeks later I left to stay in the flat of a friend of Sarah's. My stomach churning, coiling, my whole body a-tremble with anxiety and tiredness. My throat almost closed on itself with tension; all of me tired and anxious and fearful, just drained and a-tremble.

Now, as I write, I am tired and I will go away from this page to reflect and have a shower and clean myself. I do not know what I did and if I deserved what she did.

I do know there was that time a few years ago when she had done something or other again and I had said to my CPN that I would no longer accept such things. And in saying it, I realised I didn't love her anymore.

I no longer wanted to apologise or accommodate. I no longer wanted to walk along the beachfront when we retired, pushing her in her wheelchair now that we were both old and infirm. I no longer looked forward to the future. I became fake. I was not strong enough to tell her or me that I no longer loved her. I no longer lay in bed aching to be caressed. I no longer wanted to confide. I no longer shared my heart with her and yet I pretended I did. And for this I deserved all that she did.

I had always believed, with all of me, that I would spend my life with her. I had promised her this.

I had promised that I would love her until even the stars became weary. I had given her this security, this certainty that we had a life to share.

I remember one day when we decided to replace my wedding ring that had snapped in half. I remember being in a jewellery shop in Edinburgh. How I was grumpy and she didn't realise why. How I was thinking,

Don't put this on my finger, I don't want it.

But she did and she reached up to kiss me and held my hand as we walked out the shop and I was thinking;

One day I will leave you.

I remember the conversations with Sarah to try to re-find my love for my wife and how I should never have had them, and how sometimes I convinced myself the texts or the letters or the walks together would change everything but they never ever did.

They became a frantic chasing after a love that was slipping, hour by hour and minute by minute, out of my heart and my memory. So when finally I left, I should have been blissfully happy.

A part of me thought I could have that adolescence I never had, that I could learn to date and could spend nights in town and at the pub and with wonderful women. That I would sing and dance and become so much more energetic and engaged with life. But I didn't. Instead it was like a bomb went off. I woke up in a new world. A world where I had no money and no possessions. A world where I slept in a tiny flat with a kitchen in the cupboard under the staircase and where my bed was a mattress with wrinkled sheets and a smelly downie. A world where I dreaded the sound of a text, the ring of the phone, of seeing another email. A world where I left almost every friend I thought I had made behind.

It was like those 25 years or so had been zipped closed and sent off to the incinerator, never to be talked about again. Replaced with a new life where my heart lived thumping in my chest, my stomach coiling in hollow loops of anxiety, my legs always wanting to go elsewhere. I was so ignorant about the whole bit of being separate. So lost and helpless.

It took me six months to set up a new bank account and to separate our finances, and I didn't understand what my wife was saying, except that I shouldn't spend money. So I didn't.

I spent no more than £50 on my new home, getting the cheapest towels and kettles and frying pans and sheets. I bought the cheapest of the value food. I grudged every penny I spent and worried about every penny I spent.

There was one week where I had ten pence to last me for four days and always there was this assault by text and phone. My new friends told me not to look at the texts or answer the phone calls but I felt too guilty not to.

I remember throughout this time the calls would come and go, on and on and on. And I would be pleading with my wife to stop, to let me go. She would shout and shout at me and tell me how disgusting I was and how awful I was.

One time she got so cross with me she threw the phone across the room and it smashed into pieces, but ten minutes later she was phoning me back on another phone to tell me again how terrible a person I was. Ah lonely, lonely dark times.

I am not reflecting. I am not considering or pausing. I am telling the facts as I have decided they are. The wee story of how we were, the story that lets me sleep free at night.

I do not know the facts anymore. I know almost nothing.

It is midnight and the radio is recounting what all the people in parliament have been doing today. Lots of people will be indignant because people are always being indignant. I have been in the sitting room, reading the emails my wife sent me; a raw series of shrieks of abandonment. I feel vacant with the loss that I caused, I feel blank with pain.

I see extracts she has written me from a long love letter I wrote her; it took ages, and care, to write and at the time I did and did not love her but wished so much to, wished the making of the beautiful words would reach her. And in the email she says it is the most beautiful love letter ever written but I do not remember what I wrote, or even if I loved her or if I just wanted to love her, wanted it all to be all right again.

She says that just before I left her we had started to become intimate again and how could that be? But it wasn't intimacy as I know it, and when I see that sentence I know that she was reaching out from vulnerability and that great surge of strength that says,

'I will make it ok.'

And yet she couldn't.

Even as she was slowly gaining the courage to begin to touch me again, I was far, far away. Far and alone and lost and alone, and lost and needing not to be there; not pretending anymore. In those letters that I have been reading from her, I know that I was cruel and harsh and unforgiving and I know that I brought a blunt hammer into her life as surely as if I had hit her and battered her. And I know that I did the same to my son, and I know that I was naïve and illiterate in compassion or love or friendship to expect there to be anything but pain between us all. And I am sad. And I am sad because sometimes I wonder to myself,

'Was it worth it to leave all that?'

Purely because I dreaded a life where I no longer loved and begged for a life where love might become possible, where I did not wake any more to a back turned against me. I do not know and I wonder why I

41

printed so many of those emails off, saved those letters that will prey on my mind, make me think, *What did I do?* I am guilty of betrayal. I am guilty of desertion. I am sad.

And I would still do it again.

DANCING

Ah, I am filled with the missing of you and the relief of the being free of everyone. I do not understand all these things that make up love and life; the wholly messy web of it.

Sometimes there are times when I yearn to be alone, to lie in my bed, not thinking in a thinking sort of way, when I want to walk alone and read alone and eat alone. There are times when I need the room to be lazy and self-centred and full of the luxury of the space of being free to do whatever I want to do, and to think whatever I want and to be oblivious of the needs, wants, desires and insecurities of other people, even other people who I love dearly.

And yet, this morning when I was lying in bed, I was waiting for your texts. When I was making my coriander and chilli scrambled eggs I was thinking of your comments on them. And when I was about to phone you I remembered you would be watching a film with your daughter and mum and I found myself craving your company, or at least your hand in mine as we both stared at the screen above us.

It is a funny feeling, this missing you when I am treasuring every moment I have alone. I find myself seeing you in my mind. I can see your face, your lips, I can see the colour of your eyes. I can feel the touch of your skin. Just as I was thinking that, I breathed in and could smell your hair when I lean over to cuddle you.

While I was reading my book I could hear your children laughing, see them bouncing with you, crawling over you.

I want to hear your voice, I want to lose that slight melancholy that I get in my spirit when I am alone and pick up the phone and be filled with the desire to, I don't know what, just communicate. Communicate all these half-understood, half-felt feelings.

I am playing blind man's buff and I am walking through this darkness, knowing it is you I will find and embrace with joy, but at the same time feeling a slight unease at my journey, a sense of, where am I? How do I reach out to hold tight to love and let it blossom by allowing it to be free? To let it grow by refusing to label it and possess it.

And yet I want the opposite. I want to wrap love in a pretty box and treasure it and preserve it, and peek in each time I feel an absence, little knowing that by confining it, I introduce doubt into it.

It is very hard to dance when you have no sense of rhythm and uncoordinated feet, and yet dance I must, with that lightness that keeps a sunbeam stronger than ever I could be. Dance I must, to know how to love and how to relax and how to trust and how to smile without a reckoning in the back of my mind.

Dance I must and dance I will, and you have given this to me.

ALL IN HOW WE SEE IT

It all gets a wee bit confusing when I talk about mental illness, mainly because people say that I don't have insight into what my 'illness' is, but such a thing, for me, is very fluid.

I know loads about mental illness, though if you asked me to define the characteristics of different illnesses, I couldn't.

I know that some of my beliefs are not shared by others. I almost know that some of my beliefs are wrong, are, in fact, a sign of illness and yet at the same time, I know that this is incorrect.

I know, really, that the core part of me is that I am evil. That I have spirits warping me and that I might in fact be a devil, is true. I cannot escape from it.

I hate being evil and I hate having an illness that makes me believe I am evil, and I hate that I spend hours trying to work out what bit is true. The more I think of my evil, the more powerful it becomes. It gains a force in my heart and takes me over.

And when it takes me over, I know that I am the root of the evil around us and know that I need to get rid of me, get rid of me to save the world and my friends.

That's when I end up in hospital.

The less I think about it and the happier I am, the less power the devil has, but when I am like that and I am happy being me, at the back of my mind I am always worrying, worrying about the evil that must be spilling from me. Thinking, *the more selfish I am, ignoring my evil, the more the evil will get out. That if I had some strength and willpower I would get rid of myself to stop me destroying the joy of the people all around me.*

But then I take my hands and push it down away from me and try not to look at it. Try to ignore it.

That's the main part. The bit that means people gather around me to look after me. There are other bits.

Sometimes I can tell that people can read my thoughts. It's all a bit silly really. I will be sitting down with people and will suddenly know that they know what I am thinking. As a result I find it impossible not to think bad thoughts about them. I might make sexual comments to them or insult them or say something I know will hurt them, and these thoughts will be swirling through my mind and I will be thinking to myself,

I am so sorry. I don't mean to, I do apologise.

And I will be looking at them, feeling grateful that they are polite enough to ignore what I am thinking, to stay neutral about what I am doing. Sometimes I wonder if I am the only person in the world who is not telepathic.

Sometimes I wonder if people talk about me behind my back when I have been commenting on them in my head. Talking to each other, discussing the horrid things I think and then I curl up a bit with embarrassment.

In the past, when that happened more often, I would have this thing where, in my mind, I would erect a barbed wire barricade to my thoughts and theirs and I would send rose petals everywhere, wafting apologies to them, blocking the thoughts.

I *have* heard voices but I think the voices I hear are not much like the voices some people hear; they do not harass me or molest me. I hear them as loud as if someone was sitting next to me. Sometimes it is someone calling my name or it is the doorbell ringing, or it is my phone ringing or someone else being called. Occasionally it is so real that I get up to answer the door or look at my phone.

Away back in the past I would hear music that wasn't there. I would sit still and hear entire symphonies or something like that.

All that used to happen when I was tired and stressed. The same applied to when I saw things. I saw ghosts in hospital when I was tired; sheets and wraps of white light wafting round the room but then I was exhausted. And then, when I was much younger, the lights in the room

46

or the sparks of light on the sea could turn into spirits and those spirits would be beaming thoughts into my head, warping my thinking, messing it up, confusing me.

Then there is the silence, the emptiness, this inability to find anything to say, this lack of emotion. I can't describe it properly. I often feel like I am a computer that has crashed and only know this because on occasion I almost wake up, feel the world around me, feel an exhilaration at being alive and with people, and then I seem to fall, fall into a morass where there just seems to be so little that is actually there.

I used to think that being mentally ill made me romantic and interesting, someone to talk about and look at with curiosity, but now I am fed up with it. I prefer the idea of being free of these realities and beliefs. I prefer the idea of just being ordinary and normal and doing everyday things.

I've just been talking with a good friend, Joan, about her view of psychosis and that it is a spiritual awakening. And I remember a speech, a wonderful speech that Sheena did on the same subject.

A bit of me is very jealous. I would like the courage to open my belief into the knowledge that these experiences do not have to be all about impairment and tragedy. I would like to step outside of medicine and caution and to believe in the multitude of realities and experiences we can go through. I would like to believe with all my heart that my experiences are real and yet I am terrified to go there, terrified of going back into evil.

I do not want to have to kill myself. I do not want to face that. I want to keep some of my joy with me. Unlike them, I want, more than anything, to believe that I really do have schizophrenia; to know without doubt. If I could know that my world was false, I could relax, I could see new solutions, I could find a brighter and softer, more loving reality.

Oh! It does get a wee bit boring listing the different experiences I go through.

A little slice of history, maybe almost some case notes...

I was first referred to a psychologist when I was 17 but refused to see him and I was first admitted to a psychiatric hospital when I was twenty. At that time I was diagnosed with borderline personality disorder. After some chaotic years and then some lovely years, I was next admitted to hospital when I was 28, just after my son was born. That was when I was sectioned for the first time. For the next two years I didn't do too well. It was then that I was diagnosed with schizophrenia. And then there is a gap, I really can't remember it too well now. I was on medication but pretty happy for maybe twelve years, maybe even longer. I went into hospital again and I think my son would have been 13 or 14. Around this time I think they wondered if maybe I had psychotic depression or schizoaffective disorder instead but I am not too sure. Whatever it was, I have been in hospital two or three times since then and each time I have been sectioned. At some point my psychiatrist came to a firm diagnosis of paranoid schizophrenia, or at least that is what it says on my paperwork from the tribunals I attend when appealing my section. And attached to that is depression and anxiety. I get the anxiety and depression bit but not the schizophrenia part.

My depression. Actually, though I say I do, I don't really get it. I take my Fluoxetine most of the time. I am usually very active, very dynamic, very engaged with what I do. But sometimes I find a cloak of weariness around me. A dark shadow, and I become exhausted and just so, so negative. It is like that spark goes and I cannot see anything positive in anything.

When that happens, I sleep badly. I begin to look after myself less, I begin to drink more, the house gets untidy and I become irritable and sad and always I find the tears gathering in my throat. And usually I don't notice I am tired or sad and I don't notice that I am ultra-serious and becoming obsessed with my work. It does seem to me that when I don't take my antidepressants that my mood gets worse but I don't really know.

And my anxiety; well, that is the nights thinking and thinking and unable to switch off; it is my juddering legs and becoming fixated on what people have said and done or not done. The insecurity and fear of those around me, who doubt me. It is that constant worry about what people think of me, and that constant worry about how to speak to and interact with other people. Looking at people and knowing that they can see how bad and awful I really am. And knowing that people do avoid me, do feel uncomfortable in my company, though they deny it. It is deciding I am ill in so many ways.

At the moment I am sure I am dying of cancer. I have a pain in my back and sometimes I have a cough. I have a lot of wind and a lump on my shin and another on my heel. I've an ulcer in my mouth that keeps recurring. I'm not sure what I've got; some combination of lung cancer, throat, mouth and foot cancer! I'm not actually sure that I am dying of cancer but I put a lot of thought into it.   Enough thought that I don't want to tell anyone about it unless I make it into a joke.

And on the subject of wind, I swallow air all the time at the moment and just as I have a mouth guard to stop me grinding my teeth, I assume that this is anxiety too. And then there is the fear of how I have acted and how other people have acted, and the mountain of doubt that I can put around me in social situations. Like yesterday; I met Mary, had a nice conversation but kept trying to leave because I felt she was just putting up with me. I nearly got into trouble because she began to think I didn't want to be with her, when I did. I was just certain that I had overstayed my welcome in the first five minutes together.

I can't think of any more signs of 'mental illness' at the moment. I've mentioned all this as a sort of setting the scene thing, a sort of 'this may make him interesting' thing. I don't know why it should, but I hope it does.

For most of the time I am not living with that life. I do not spend my every waking moment in an agony of the worst sort. No. Usually I'm ambling around, watching telly, working, walking on the beach, talking to friends, cooking meals, just being very, very ordinary and normal.

Far too boring for my liking, but generally just ambling along, a wee bit monotonously.

When I last left hospital some years ago, I made myself a promise that I would learn to see beauty. Treasure it, find joy in the scent of the wind on my face.

I felt delicate and brand new, as though after my long stay in the stale warm air, with the constant cleanliness and the continual chatter of the television and the mass-produced food, I had breathed in a brand new life with brand new bright eyes and a soft, fresh mind.

Being able to go home and being able to do whatever I wanted to do, go to sleep whenever I felt the need, knowing no one would open the door to check I was safe. I could drink wine, cook meals of fresh vegetables, talk to my friends, see the young children and the dogs and the seagulls. It felt like I had gone to sleep in a meadow and woken up bathed in dew, washed clean so that my eyes sparkled. I looked at my body and thought,

It is alive!

I looked at my friends and said,

'They smile at me!'

I looked at the sea and it danced in the sun. I wanted to touch my fingers to my lips and say,

'This is warm, is able to speak, is filled with breath and the rush of blood that keeps me soft and smooth and vibrant.'

It reminded me of that moment I was first taken off 'constant observations'. The following first few hours I must have seemed so silly. I kept getting up from my seat and sitting on another seat and no one would follow me. I would walk round the corridors of the ward alone and no one commented.

I giggled. I walked into my room and saw that the chair with the magazines had gone. I closed the door. I closed the door and no one rushed to see what was happening. I pulled the cover over my face and no one said, 'Stop that!'

I went to the toilet and no one insisted I keep the door open to check on me. I was just so delighted, so full of a face-stretching smile. I was free. In my room, at night, I was allowed to shut the curtains, turn off the light and sit staring into the darkness. The darkness that I had been forbidden to rest in, for fear of what I would do. Wow! Wonderful. So wonderful.

The contrast reminds me of when I went for my tribunal. The tribunal that would decide on my freedom, the tribunal everyone said I would lose. That even I said I would lose.

Walking through the ward door with my escort, watching that door swing shut behind me and thinking,

I am free of that air, of the same chairs and people and coffee mugs.

Passing the patients' paintings on the walls. Turning the corner at the end of the corridor, there is not the slightest sound of an alarm. My feet are walking confidently, happily. I am not running, my heart thumping in my chest, the staff rushing after me. Walking up to the main door. No one is dashing out the office. I am not stopped at it, scrabbling at its edges, prising it open so that I can get out, so that I can escape.

Walking into the car park. No cars are slewing to a halt in front of me, their doors bouncing open as the off-duty nurses see me running. No, I am walking calmly and slowly and I am smiling.

I am looking up at the sun, at the clouds, I am walking over the grass. The grass! Feeling the bark of a tree before pausing in front of the car. This is wonderful!

Looking at the dirt, the birds. Looking at the bent grass, the grit left on the road from the last snow, there is the breeze on my face and away over there, are people walking and cars driving.

In the car I have to promise not to do anything dangerous. I am told that the child locks will be on. I don't care. We drive through town – people, cars, pictures, shops, the river. Yay! This is wonderful. I am a fifty-year-old child with my nose stuck to the windscreen.

We cannot get parked at the tribunal office, so we have to park in the garden centre where there are flowers and more grass and the freedom of putting one step in front of the other in the fresh air.

Ah! Here's Sarah. Here to represent my best interests that are not my interests and to give me time for a brief hug, and a wee suggestion from me that maybe it would be better, now that I am here, to run, run, run away, which she relays to my nurse.

My nurse tells me how quickly the police would be here, how quickly I would be caught, how horrid I would find it, and I walk inside.

A clerk, a small man, all cheery, offers me sweeties, greets me, laughs. I am not sure whether to feel patronised or delighted.

A person I work with pokes his head out the door, sees me, says, 'Hello.'

And goes back inside.

We joke and giggle at the long, long polished table, get confused, have things explained to us. The tribunal members file in. I used to work with one of them occasionally. We get more confused, have more things explained to us, do some more joking.

The psychiatrist and mental health officer explain why they think I am ill, why I should be detained for six months, why I am a threat to myself or even others, why and why and why.

And it is like their words are lumps of concrete falling from the sky on me, battering me, embarrassing me, making me look at the table.

Everyone thinks differently to me, sees me differently to how I see me. The force of their words is a mountain of concrete blocks and I am no longer laughing and my feet are jiggering up and down and then it is my turn.

It is hard to repeat words that you know no one will listen to, hard to speak up, to appear confident. Hard to explain, hard to explain why they should let me die, that if they understood they would see it was their duty to – Oh, I forget now – imprison me in concrete shelters, drain my blood and incinerate it, keep the world free from my evil.

I grin as I talk; I do not know what else to do. I ache in my heart with humiliation.

When the tribunal members are gone, we talk amongst ourselves, eat some more sweets. I ask after Cara and Sally, chatter to my MHO and my nurse.

They come back, all solemn, take their places and their papers and their pens and their glasses of water, tell me they appreciate my opinion but that they cannot agree to do what I want and that they agree to the detention. And when they are gone my nurse says that was the fastest decision she has ever seen, and we laugh and I hug Sarah goodbye.

In the car park I rub the trees, feel the soil under my feet, get in the car, watch the world go by, the people walking carefree with shopping bags and prams and children.

We cross the canal. Drive back into the hospital car park. I walk to the ward, down the corridors. Back to the nurses who never leave my side, back to the square that the ward circles, the square of light in the courtyard outside. The chair at my door, the open door, the pile of magazines, the shadow person who follows me everywhere. I lie on my bed, careful not to cover myself too much, not to have too much of me out of sight and my heart is empty, all slow and silent and lost and lonely. Wondering if this will ever end.

When I think of freedom I think to myself, 'But I am a wee bit lost.'

People live and die and spend their lives pursuing freedom, searching for it, yearning for it, praying for it and I don't know what it is.

I think perhaps that I am so used to being free, to being able to write things like this without fear, to walk where I want, think what I want, to sleep when I want, that I do not know, have no knowledge what it is like to be in a place where I am not free.

People say, 'You have to let your CPN in through the door. You have to arrive every two weeks for your injection and if you refuse the police will be called, it will be forced on you. You have to say where you live, you have to see your psychiatrist and your mental health officer.'

They say, 'Are you not angry? Does it not weigh on you?'

And I do not understand. I like my CPN. I can talk to her, she gives me good advice, she listens to me. I like my psychiatrist, even though he is ever so young and almost incoherent in his awkwardness. My new MHO is warm and kind and gentle and, once every two weeks, I wander up the road for a wee jag. Is that so terribly bad?

I suppose *Guardian* readers like me could see me as Arthur at the end of *1984*, craving Big Brother and the system, but to me it is insignificant.

There are rules everywhere. If I don't turn up at work I will have no income; if I don't fill in the right forms every year I won't be able to drive. If I don't pay my mortgage I will have nowhere to live. Well, wait a moment, for me that's not true. I suspect that because I am probably seen as vulnerable I would be rehoused the moment I lost my home.

And then all those rules of appearance. If I dress a certain way I will be seen a certain way and treated a certain way; if I laugh at the wrong moments, or cry in the wrong way, make the wrong sort of jokes, dislike the wrong groups of people. If I argue too much, love too much, talk to children who are not related to me, lie down on a bench or on the pavement, read a book at a party; if I make faces, wash too infrequently; if I talk too much or say exactly what I think, or tell a story at a meeting or dance at a conference. If I like the wrong people or have an untidy house, decide I don't want to work or decide I want to work all the time; if I interrupt or argue too much. If I don't listen or am far too intense. If I paint my house with polka dots or let my garden (which I don't have) get overgrown with nettles, talk all the time or never ever talk. If I do these things or myriad, myriad other things, I will find my neighbours ignore me, my friends try to change me, my acquaintances avoid me, my family discuss me, my employers monitor me, the community make up a nickname for me.

I will find myself slowly discarded, slowly let go. I will gently find myself alone, people will avert their eyes, they will stop being honest with me. People will tell other people to avoid me and slowly the telly will replace people for conversation, and all those webs that bind us together will be snipped through, one by one, and I will be alone.

If I am lucky, professionals will step in to provide companionship, but they will write up notes of each encounter and each sentence will highlight my inadequacy. Christmases will come and go and I will see no one, and I think to myself, 'What do we mean by freedom?'

This is not the state, this is us. This is our community, excluding each other, leaving people like us discarded and alien and lost, and at this point I think, 'What do we mean by freedom?'

When people say, 'You must be so angry!'

I think seeing my CPN for an hour does not compare to imprisonment. People talk of Russia or Syria or Iran or China and I do not know these countries or these systems. I have almost never feared who may come to my door, who may monitor my phone calls, ask my neighbours about me.

I have never feared this and do not know what it means, but I do know the blank terror at the fear of the disintegration of myself if my community gathers into its breast its collective values, its ways of interacting, its mechanisms of communication and, if it wishes, walks past me with a blank look, gazes at my face with a stony smile, takes away my job, questions my support, re-evaluates me and has case conferences about me. And then I think, *I have learned how to be free but only if I follow the rules that limit our freedom.*

I know how to speak, how to dress, how to eat, what to believe and what to say about what I believe. I know when to get my injection. I know the rules. Does that make me free or am I an ant following the ant in front of me, turning on the ants that are different to me?

Freedom seems to be a meaningless word to people such as me, who have never had to watch what they say on the phone or who they mix with on the street. Freedom. I do not know it.

I am not free of me, I am not free of my past, I am not free of my mistakes or my memories. I am not free of the loving web that my friends and acquaintances and family build about me.

It makes me think of this thing called independence that all these well-meaning policymakers say is the ultimate aim of our support. I do not understand this. To me, true independence is an arid, lonely, bitter world where you only believe in your own path, where you are so arrogant that you follow only your vision, make your own rules.

It is that one bedroom house you inhabit to stare at the telly and sleep through the day, in between the weekly visits from your helpers who feel a sense of failure because you are not dancing at your autonomy, not transforming yourself into a fully employed, fully productive, talkative, included, normal person.

I prize my interdependence; when I get stuck in a thought, someone challenges me, when I am trying to shape an opinion, I listen to another person or read the latest newspaper. When I decide on a certain form of behaviour I adapt it to the world I live in, and when I think about how I am going to live, I think of the sea. I think of charity shops and families, I think of cooking meals together. I think of that web of connection that makes us community.

A community where the actions of one person influence and shape the actions of another, where each thought, each hour, jiggles the web we have in such a way that we all live a long complicated interdependent dance.

When we are caught in the system and stuck in empty houses we can be said to be independent and that can be seen as success. But I think of the people I know, who talk about the stomach-churning loneliness, the poverty, the spaces where thoughts grow and grow, way out of control because there is no one to share them with. No one to test them with. So that an innocent greeting can, by the end of the week, be seen as a dire insult.

Independence where, unlike most people, the weekend is the lowest part of the week, the time everywhere shuts, where you do not utter a word unless it is to the empty air.

Maybe the aim of independence is being independent of support, because our world is one of economics. Because when we are discharged, when our support is reduced we are seen as successes. Because on the one hand we are meant to recover, and damn us to hell if we don't make the best of our lives in the presence or absence of symptoms, and on the other hand we have life-long disabilities and illnesses tainted by that edge of judgement. That hint of derision that says:

If you were just, just, just… well, if you just did this, you wouldn't be who you are. You wouldn't be the burden you are. If you just… you would be like us: working, dancing, looking after parents and children. Have you not understood what we try to tell you? You can recover. You can embark on the journey to productivity, you can make that journey.

And maybe we can, but do we really want to? Are we your model pawns, seeking out the best way to conform, the best way to fit into your system of productivity and that painful, painful positivity?

56

There are those people who say that mental illness is not really mental illness, is not really disability, there is that wee hint that we do not quite believe in it. That we quite like those old books such as *The Myth of Mental Illness or Toxic Psychiatry*. That the social model of disability trumps the medical one each time. That our only disability is society.

Sometimes I wonder how people with cerebral palsy or spina bifida would feel if they had this constant undertow that says, 'You don't really have this condition. If you just work hard at it, it will all slip off your shoulders and you will be the shiny-eyed person we always knew you could be.'

Sometimes I wonder why there is this relentless emphasis on hope and positivity, on responsibility and our strengths and assets, when for many of us, the simple existence of a friendly face is so rare, and joy so elusive, that to dare that leap into the future seems so frightening and dangerous.

Do these people not feel like born-again evangelists, promising us blinkered sinners a light in our eyes, if only we opened our minds to the hope they offer us? Taking control and growing is so much more than the trite sentences of recovery and mutuality, the knee jerk rejection of psychiatry, the continual stereotyping of people who help us when we so earnestly plead to be free of that self-same labelling.

I get so confused at all these reports from the United Nations that seem to utterly reject mental illness. The reports that say that even when someone can no longer speak or make a decision of any sort that they should still be in control of all that happens to them, have the final say, even though they stare blankly at the wall, not speaking, not reacting, not eating or dressing. This form of independence does feel just like another telling of *The Emperor's New Clothes*, where idealism and naivety replace the evidence of what is in front of our faces.

Maybe independence is being free of our workers? It is perhaps here that the greatest offense lies.

Our workers have 'boundaries'. Our workers are never allowed to be our friends, our workers sometimes feel that it is unprofessional to acknowledge us if they see us in the street. Will sometimes only disclose

57

bits of their lives to us if it is seen to enhance the therapeutic relationship. Our workers will never do things socially with us. Will face disciplinary action if they communicate out of work, give us their phone number, invite us to the pub. Can be sacked if they give us a comforting hug. And yet:

We spend years and years with them. They share our joys and sorrows, they keep us from the abyss and yet accompany us there if we slip off its edge. They know more about us than our lovers or family. They hear us when we have lost everything and they help pick us up. They celebrate our joy at the steps we make. They spend ages discussing us with strangers, they monitor our diet and our exercise. They help us to change our lives, from something that may seem unliveable, to its opposite. And yet if, when they have done something particularly good, we rush across the room to give them a thank you hug, the barriers come up, the shutters in their eyes come down.

We spend years developing a trust in them, a joy in them, a sharing of our lives and then at the point where we feel we can walk our first steps, we lose them and never see them again when we are discharged. They can shift somewhere else at almost no notice and we wake to learn to trust a new stranger all over again, waiting until they move on in turn. Waiting until a case conference decides we are too dependent on them and that we need less time with them; that the relationship is bad for us

March

LATE SPRING IN APPLECROSS

The suck of the sunset sea on the rocks and boulders at our feet. In the blue patch of the darkening sky, the lighthouses of Rhona and Raasay blink across the sound.

The taste of your lips, the taste of the spicy chocolate, making jokes, giggling. The window goes black and reflects us back at ourselves. In the Sound, small ships pass north and south and the occasional helicopter scratches across the sky.

Bright room, a blue bed and mirrors, lightness. You sat on the white couch, twisting your hair, reading travel books.

Listening to Sheryl Crow, Macy Gray, Portishead, Rihanna. Making noises like the Clangers. Giggling.

Waiting for the heaters to warm the room. Thinking of the old croft on the seashore. Practising walking on your knees on the slab of rock.

'Ow! That hurts!'

Wondering why children always have scuffed knees. Watching the seaweed lift and twist in the swell of the waves. Giggling and kissing.

Drinking cut-price malt whisky 'cos it's the holidays. Thinking, *it's cold outside*.

Wondering where the stars are.

Remembering the moss-covered boulders of ruined houses at Applecross, the dark gloom of the forest.

Pondering a shower. Thinking you could join me there. We would giggle and soap each other.

In the far distance a car's red tail light appears and disappears on the single track coastal road.

Feeling glad the hill from Lochcarron was closed. That we drove along the coast with the burn of the golden light in our eyes. The silver sea and the white mountains and a fire in the woods and you writing 'GMo's car' in the dirt on the door.

Both of us giggling, pressing our cold faces together, feeling our warm lips.

The delicate shell of an egg breaking, letting us share in the birth of tiny adventures together.

Knowing the sound of your laugh. The trust in your hands as you caress me.

Daring to make fools of ourselves together because we don't know how that could ever hurt us.

Building a history of stories that only we will understand.

Giggling at, 'Respect the bitch, don't diss her!'

Giggling at our return to childhood humour. Sharing kisses and a blanket. Listening to Adele and Sandy Denny.

Charging our phones even though there is no signal. Wondering if we will see sea eagles.

Wondering when the landlady will arrive, whether she will want to talk to us. Maybe have a whisky with us.

Thinking, *Will the road be icy tomorrow?*

Giggling inside at the thought of us cuddling in bed and the sheep peering through the window at our naked feet poking out of the covers.

Listening to Ali Farka Touré. Wondering when to have tea and whether to watch TV.

Remembering my wallet is in the unlocked car and that the nearest person is a mile away.

Giggling at you saying, 'Hello,' to me from the couch, two feet away.

Remembering the spiral of a buzzard, the elongated blackness of a cormorant, two silent trails in the loch from ducks, and the dumpy clatter of a grouse.

Listening to Janis Joplin. Wishing I could text photos to friends of the blue sky, the boulders, the wool-encrusted heather.

Thinking, *you will all be giggling because a short while ago I was saying I will never love, never trust, never hurt, never dare to dream, to share, to dance with my fingers on another person's skin.*

Never in a hundred years will I take that step that joins me to the world again and now I am inviting you, my love, to parties – the woman lying on the couch a couple of feet away, twirling her hair, laughing at my choice in music.

Drinking tea, making lemon drizzle cake, daring to giggle the day away, to have kisses where hair gets in our mouths.

Making a spiral of fingertips, tracing patterns on our skin.

Giggling because we know we are fragile, that we are leaping off a cliff in the bright blue day, with snow on the mountains, and an evening tucked up, comforted by the dark blue-black and the stars.

Knowing that leap is all we can do and if we land hard or soft, we will have flown for a time together, giggling all the while.

WHY HAVE YOU FORSAKEN ME?

I do not have words to express this part of my story. I will try. I will search for the right expression, the appropriate phrase, but I cannot do this because I cannot even tell it to myself. I know the facts but they sit in a great big maw of incomprehension. It just sits there gaping wide, making me think one day those claws will snap about me, sweep me down to the place, the place of I-know-not-what, but it is somewhere I would do anything to avoid. I see the facts and sometimes I try to write about them, sometimes I try to describe him or remember him, but I cannot do it, I just fail at the first hurdle.

When I was twenty and busy hating my dad and my upbringing, I had this oath, this promise I made to myself. I promised myself that no child of mine would ever go through what I went through, no child would grow up hating me, detesting me. I would pour love into my child, I would treasure him and cosset him and show that love, bring that presence, that joy I would feel about him, into his life. I would do everything so that he could grow up with friends and confidence. He would be happy to dance and sing, he would do things for the sake of doing them. He would not be lonely, he would not be frightened and he would not be angry in the same way I was.

And I sort of thought that I had done a good job, that between us everything had worked out sort of ok. I thought that despite his grumps, his taunts and attitude, he loved me, treasured me a wee bit. Maybe not as much as I had wanted but good enough for a middle-aged man and his teenage son.

And he did seem to have so much in his life that I had wanted him to have; the friends, the cleverness, the excitement. I was wrong. What I had dreaded more than anything else, my nightmare, the thing that would make me think I had got everything wrong, happened.

It is four years, well, four and half years since he has spoken to me, in fact four and half years since he has communicated with me in any way. Well, no, I lie. Four years and three months ago he sent me a Post-it in his mum's letter that said, 'Never write to me again.'

His mum told me that he thought of me as a dead person, that he wanted to never see me again or hear from me or speak to me. She said that although he was accepting of mental illness, that mine was beyond the pale, that people like me were unacceptable, unmentionable.

I tell a lie. Three and a half years ago, I think, on Christmas day, his mum phoned me when I was in hospital and spoke to me, and at one point she got him to agree to let me listen to him playing his piano. I couldn't hear his voice or his breathing, I couldn't see him, but I could hear his music. Hearing his music was one of my most wonderful, wonderful, experiences.

I cannot emphasise just how happy I was in the past to sit on the sofa, listening to him play away on the keyboard or the Clavia, or whatever it was. I never understood what he was doing but I think it was called improvisation, and seeing him and hearing the music filled me with a pride and a joy I had never ever known in anyone before.

Hearing him play that Christmas while the nurse who was observing me sat outside my room with a Santa hat on and I opened my single present of shampoo, supplied courtesy of the hospital, made my day. Made me soft with delight.

Christmas in hospital is not good. The nurses all had a Christmas breakfast in front of us, with the ones doing 'constant obs' being relieved from their duties long enough to have their fry up. We were not given anything exciting at breakfast. The kitchen was still open for us to have toast and butter and tea but that was it.

The ward was decorated and very quiet because anyone who could possibly go home had been sent home. I would still have been on hunger strike at that time. It would have been my third week of not eating. The one good thing about it was that I no longer needed to go to the toilet so it was less embarrassing using the loo.

The day was boring. I think I spent the early hours feeling totally alone, sending desperate texts to friends I thought I had, who unsurprisingly, mainly didn't reply at all and if they did, mostly didn't reply until the morning. It would have been snowy, if I have the correct admission. The rooftops of the ward bulging with layers of whiteness, the courtyard piled high with snow and cigarette butts and I would walk round and round it, wearing my icy path in the snow while the nurse watched from just by the door.

Not long after I was admitted, one night, when that young nursing assistant was 'specialling' me, I was lying in my bed, the ward quiet, the lights in my room turned low when it grabbed me.

My son, my son, my son. I cannot, cannot do this. Why have you done this? Why do you hate me? Why do you hate me? Why did your mum refuse to let me take away any photos of her or you? Saying that if I didn't want to be with her anymore, I had no right to any image of either her or you? I want to hold you, I want to be teased by you. I want to see you, see your beautiful eyes, your thick curly hair, your olive skin.

I would even be ecstatic if you turned the corner and gave me another of those playful punches that leave dark bruises on my arm. I would be over the moon if you would repeat your refrain of how you hate me because I am such a 'weirdo' and then laugh as if you half-do, half-don't mean it.

My son. I am lying in my bed and I am alone and I am aching for you, just a glimpse, a sight of what you are doing with your life, an idea of what you look like now, a hint of where you live and what you do.

Ah, lost it there! Got lost in the memory, got lost in the stuff I do not say to myself. But I remember lying in bed, my wrist still in its bandage and I started to cry and I was all alone. And the more I cried the more I wanted to cry, until I was crying in a way I had never cried before, still trying to muffle my sobs but not succeeding, feeling my stomach filled with shudders and my breath ragged, the way a child's is when it gets overwrought. Occasionally the person on the door would say something nice to me, something comforting, something that let me cry more without shame, until the rawness of my tears were flooding out of the bedroom and I was worried that I would wake and upset all the other patients.

The only good thing about all this was that I realised with such clarity what my anger and my blame had done to my mum and dad over the years. How horrible it must have been for them.

In the years when I used to sit and get drunk with my dad and tell him how harsh I had found my upbringing, he would listen to me and I can't really remember what I said to him, but I don't remember him contradicting me. I don't ever remember him saying, 'Hold on a bit, that isn't right. You've got that wrong, we never did that.'

Because I am sure I did. I am sure I did get it wrong. I am very fluid with memory and fact and history. And my dad never really said how hurt and damaged they were by the blame I piled high on them.

I would have been about 20 the first time I started self-harming and when I first took an overdose. I remember when I first told my parents how I was feeling and about being in the student hospital, they were shocked and silent and bewildered. I remember that when I was next admitted into the old, old asylum in Sheffield, I refused to allow the hospital to let my parents know and when they found out, because the hospital had sent a benefit claim form to their home, I wouldn't talk to them on the phone and wouldn't agree to let them visit me. I know that I made it clear I thought it was their fault that I had tried to kill myself. Locked in my arrogance and my youth and my self-pity, I had no idea at all what that might do to them. It didn't occur to me that they'd be hurt by me. I didn't think of those around me. It is a long time ago, but if I met the young me now, I think I might be savage with me.

Whenever I have been suicidal, I have either been convinced that I would bring something good to the people I love or just indifferent to the effect of what I do to those around me. Maybe not even indifferent, perhaps oblivious.

Many of the people I know say the same thing, which must be confusing to those who have to witness what we do to them. We sort of withdraw, become opaque, lost to you all. Morality becomes hazy, pain becomes diffuse, consequence abstract.

My sister would have been young at the time, about thirteen. She was another person I had little contact with for years and is now someone I value so, so much.

I first found out about the family reaction when she sat down with me (or went for a walk with me, I don't remember), a couple of years ago. When she told me what it was like to know that your older brother, who you were in awe of, had tried to kill himself and was in hospital. She talked about the silence in the house and how no one was able to talk about it and how no one could explain it to her and how frightened she was; how my mum took to taking long, long solitary walks on her own and how those walks went on into the evening and dinner wouldn't get made. So my dad would make it.

My sister talked about how bad Dad's attempts at a child's tea were; how the scrambled egg was green and how it was eaten in silence. And I never knew.

I don't know how I never knew. It seems incredible that I wouldn't know what I did to my family; that I never asked them. That I was incurious and unaware for decades. That I never paused and thought of my sister, still with her teddies, contemplating something so awful and being so alone and unable to communicate. That I never knew the need for space my mother had, and that I judged so harshly the whisky breath and the clumsy drunken hugs from my dad when I went to visit. It is shocking that I find the times when life has been different, are just times of my own self-obsession.

I sat with my brother and his wife recently and again, I learned things I had never known. I learned that during one of the times of awfulness, my brother and Sharon were in New Zealand, working, travelling, and when they heard what was happening they cut short their trip and came back home to be with me and I never knew this was the reason.

They both got good jobs in medicine in London and when I was in that hazy horrible place again, they gave up their work to come to Edinburgh and be near me, to help if I needed it and I never knew. I just assumed that it was all some weird coincidence. All the time I was hating me and my family.

They were recoiling like a sea anemone touched abruptly and then

70

reaching out with gentle arms like a baby, still ready to be bitten and attacked again and I never even noticed or knew. Even my dad, my dad of the whisky breath.

Last week he talked to me, talked to me of his sadness, talked to me of his upbringing, apologised to me when he didn't need to and told me that he saw himself as an emotional cripple, had thought of himself that way for years. Told me that when I rejected him all those years ago, he thought he would come up to see me, come up whether I wanted him or not, stay in a bed and breakfast until I would see him, speak to him. He told me that he was full of regret and the fact that for years, family was a side issue to work and sailing and the whole host of other things. I was moved and touched and horrified to know that if he had made that gesture at that time, I would not have accommodated it, would not have softened. And now I crave to find some way of asking them all to forgive me.

And so, do I understand my own son, forgive him, ask him to forgive me? Can I reach beyond myself and see him? I do not know. I no longer know anything very much.

Sometimes I think if he turned up on my doorstep, I wouldn't let him in. I would be all a-tremble, all frightened; all frightened he would lay a continent of accusation on me, all frightened that I wouldn't allow him to talk as long as he wanted, but would defend myself, would justify myself, would say, 'Do you know what you have done?'

And yet he is young. Young and full of passion and he has strong, strong opinions. When I lost his image I began to forget what he looks like, except for the picture I have of him at 14-years-old. He's 21 now. I might not recognise him in the street. It was such a privilege to be part of his life, of his humour, his quietness, his I-don't-know. There was something I was in awe of, a 'how can someone so amazing have any connection to me'? Sometimes it made me awkward with him, that sense that I didn't really live up to what I saw in him. I was so frightened, the first few years of his life when he seemed to have no friends and yet that changed. Before I left, he seemed to be surrounded by people.

When my wife seemed to decide that there would be no more

connection and no contact, he began to fade into a raw throbbing wound from which my spirit and my belief in I-don't-know-what vanished. I cannot see it, that wound. I cannot feel it. I know it gapes in my heart, sends me into coldness and silence, and vacuous grins and meaningless words when people say one day he will get in touch. I don't know.

I know so little. I cannot fathom life or what we do to each other, or what I do to people. I had always thought I was friendly and well meaning. A bit too cautious, a bit too shy, a bit too prone to alcohol and doom. But I thought he liked me. I even thought he loved me, that I was integral.

Maybe that is it. Because I left at such a point and he and my wife weren't integral to me, I did not really know the wound I made. I only knew the wound I felt my wife had made of me: the impossibility of continuing.

I just didn't know that it would be like a scimitar had extracted my adult life from me. Made the past a fading story with no joint memories to share with people. I thought we would still be friends, or at least would talk to each other and see each other. I did not know I would be walking out of one life and into a new one where there was not the slightest shred of connection. And he fades.

I don't know how to tell the story about how he insisted on holding our hands and kissing us and telling us he loved us for so long that we worried he would get teased and yet we secretly basked in it.

In knowing he loved us, was innocent and natural and affectionate.

Knowing he loved us, would talk to us and tell me stories that I would write on the computer for him. Knowing he would demand I tell him the story of the boy with red slippers, every night when I put him to bed until I ran out of things to make up. That, for ages, when I cuddled him to sleep, I would wake up an hour or so later, having nodded off next to him. Remembering he would be filled with that curiosity, that wonder, that bravery and excitement and strength and integrity. And now he hates me. Or I fear he does. Rejects me utterly. Or I fear he does. I don't really know whether he hates me still, sees me as dead to him or is just indifferent. I suppose these can only be my interpretations. Maybe he misses me, maybe he still loves me, wants to talk to me; I cannot know what he might be feeling, it is not possible in this absence to know.

But he might not love me and I don't feel I can share in his stories because they are no longer my stories anymore. They have been thrown away, and I am scared that the flock of memory is fading until all that will be, is the hurt of losing the memory of the hurt. I am sad now.

I gave a speech, my speech which mentioned him and the sadness, and is it wrong? I do not know if it is wrong. At the end of the speech, I talked of my son, talked of my son to 150 social workers. I do not know. Am I using my stories in the wrong way?

After speeches like that you usually have people come up to say,

'Thank you',

To say,

'That was superb.'

And then you wander round afterwards while people get coffee and you don't know what to do because people don't know what to do with you. But as I was wandering around feeling lonely, feeling a bit like–

Why do I do this?

A man I had never met put out his arm and stopped me, said that when he left his wife, his wife had stopped all contact with his children, that his children didn't want to speak to him until they were grown up, with children of their own and that now he treasured every moment he had with them, celebrated his life anew.

As I went up the stairs, off to a workshop, someone I had known many years ago came up to me, talked to me, wouldn't stop talking. His eyes were glistening with tears, his voice was breaking. I thought he would collapse in front of everyone passing by. He told the same story, of leaving his wife and how for a decade his daughters would say not a word to him, how it was worse to him than being dead, worse than anything he could have imagined. And that now, in the last few years, they were able to speak with him again, share their lives with him, how that is wonderful.

We grinned at how unhelpful it is when people say they are sure our children will come around, and I felt, yes, it is an ache in me, a thing that if I were able to face it, I would be leaning over the toilet bowl being sick, again and again and again.

I suppose my son may read this one day and may one day say that there is no shred of understanding here about what I did. And there isn't. I don't know what I did. I don't know why he grew up to reject me. I didn't hit him. I didn't abuse him.

Isn't that silly! As if not being horrendous and criminal must make you good and lovable. I do know I often didn't know what to say to him, that the things we did on weekends bored him, that I didn't understand the hours he spent on the computer, that I never really understood or recognised his opinion of me, always brushed it aside, thought that really he would have some affection for my disorganisation, my clumsy attempts at affection.

I expect he hated my arguments with his mum but then, he didn't hate her for having them with me. I dread to think what he may say to me. I dread to think how little I say to myself about this, how little I see of how he saw me. And I have to remind myself that it was me who left, me who walked out the house. I was leaving my wife, I thought, but it turned out I was also leaving my son as well. What else could he think of that?

BEING MINDFUL

What a day! Blue sky with frost and sunshine and wood smoke. These are my favourite days; when we wander around clutching hands, cheeks slightly fizzy with the cold, lips a bit chapped, the odd scrap of steam escaping when we breathe.

Findhorn is one of my routine trips out on the weekend. I try to avoid all the alternative people, mainly because I do not know how to speak them, but I do love the houses. I love the weird shapes they are: the hobbit houses, the caravans, the eco villas. I love the Phoenix Café, especially if it is hot enough to sit at one of the tables outside, and much as I wish I didn't, I do feel slightly superior!

I like buying seaweed from the shop and tempeh and all the exotic foods, but I do remember the last time we were there we saw this collection of people walking mindfully. I'm sure that they found it intensely liberating, and I am sure it is far better than my fortnightly depot injection, but walking past people taking thirty seconds to lift a foot off the ground, walking in a multitude of directions, but in straight lines, smiles on their faces, absolute silence. They really did look very strange, much as I imagine zombies might do.

I like that I can laugh at them, safe in the knowledge that whatever they were doing also brought them benefit, just as walking to the beach with Wendy, Jean, her boyfriend and the dog has brought us benefit. Walking by the frost-covered gorse bushes, feeling that slight shock that the sand is solid and then playing, walking round and round the double spiral of stones that someone has built at the very edge of the beach and the sea.

In the tiny bazaar, we find a treasure trove of things to take away. I get a huge candle that just nestles its base into my large coat pocket. Jean gets some boots and I think her boyfriend takes a cd. I keep intending to take things back as my own gift one day, but only rarely do so.

Wendy tells us later that she is shocked at our behaviour; she thinks we are stealing and doesn't know that the things kept there are free to take. I love that I can laugh at her because I know different, but it is not so long since I felt the same; I worried when I went in, looked through the boxes and the books that someone would come in and throw me out for being an imposter.

I wonder if I am an imposter now, walking hand in hand, looking forward to when we next cuddle up on the sofa, looking forward to the rest of the weekend, wishing I didn't have to take you to the bus tomorrow afternoon for your long journey home.

PLEADING FOR OUR INCARCERATION!

Well, what is it all about? Being on a compulsory community treatment order?

To be honest, it's no problem.

Some people try to liberate me. Many people say such things are the sign of a system clamping down on us, restricting us, oppressing us, grinding our spirit and our liberty into a terrible mess on the ground.

At an international level, committees are campaigning for a complete halt to detention and I feel an anger in me at their ignorance. I think they sigh, heave a shudder that some people like me are so taken in by the system, so unenlightened.

It makes me nervous, and a wee bit angry. I see their messages on Facebook and see people caught in a world of anger and theory, and the liberation of the anger of oppression and the ideology of oppression, and I shudder that they claim to serve to promote my rights and my freedom.

But my lack of anger and my acceptance shames me. I think I should cast myself back thirty years to when I thought as they thought.

I expect I feel like a Tory must feel at a hunt saboteurs meeting.

What happens?

I get my jag. The nurses are nice. At first I was a bit irritated that I had to go. A bit inclined to be resentful. Nowadays we talk of their families and their holidays and I talk of my day. It takes a couple of minutes. Quite often I forget to go. People say, 'How can you do that? You use your diary all the time. You never miss any other appointment. It's not possible to forget.'

But I do. I will get a call in the middle of the day and suddenly I will remember.

'Oh yuck!' and 'Oh sorry!' I say.

And then, either that day or the next, someone from the mental health team will give me a jag instead or the surgery will rejig its appointments to see me. It has to be done within a certain time or something will be triggered that means something is recorded about my compliance, or something or other. I'm not sure what.

I see my CPN every two weeks, or sometimes once a week depending on how I am doing. She's lovely. She sometimes challenges what I say about our conversations as she says they are not completely accurate. Which I think is probably true.

I tend to say we have a running argument as to whether I have schizophrenia or whether I am evil and we don't really, but it's something we talk about a lot and which we have differing views about. At the moment we are trying to help me open my mind to the fact that certain things can be interpreted and viewed in different ways; to open my beliefs to something more fluid.

Well, not at the moment, she's been off sick for four months. But in the past she was somehow so good for me.

For me, she is someone who I can turn to with my worries. She is someone I can speak to when I think people hate me, when I am drinking too much, when I am too tired, when I am working too much. She helps me unravel the minefields I put around myself and she reminds me to take holidays to look after myself. Absolutely wonderful.

I used to hate seeing CPNs but the last two have been great. It was strange when I saw the one before last; she said she was so pleased that I had agreed to see her and that they had been hoping I would agree to see a CPN for a long time, and yet I did not know that I had been refusing their help.

I don't know whether I would have liked a replacement while she has been off sick. I would have liked someone to talk to as Christmas swung by again, with all its memories and loneliness and the need not to think at all, if at all possible.

In the last few months I became so obsessed with work that I couldn't switch off, couldn't let go, couldn't relax. Christmas has become such a *Thing*; I dread it. I cannot stop thinking of my son and what was and I cannot stand the need to be cheerful at that time of the year.

It is different, here in the Highlands. We often come across the people who treat us, in our work or socially. It makes the boundaries all that wee bit more important and that wee bit more confusing.

I saw a psychologist for a couple of years. He was really nice and I would have liked to walk along the beach with him or met him in the pub. We talked a lot. I expressed pleasure in how my thinking changed but I don't think it did. I am very good at appearing to talk about something without talking about it. I think I did that a lot with him.

I also thought that it was my evil that made him go off sick so I was quite relieved when he moved on and they said that unless I wanted to really see someone else they would discharge me.

I saw an OT for a short time after leaving hospital. It felt a bit awkward because I had worked closely with her in my working life. It was good to see her. She was also a sex therapist or something, but I was too embarrassed to say to her I would like some help in that area.

Then there was the addictions CPN I saw for a few months. I must confess I didn't pay much attention to him. I hated being breathalysed before we did anything else when we met and I didn't want to read the books and leaflets he left. I was quite relieved when he got another job.

My psychiatrist is nice, but he is so young and so awkward at speaking. It makes me awkward speaking to him. He was fab in hospital. Well, he kept me alive so that is pretty fab. He is very professional and non-judgemental. It feels a wee bit weird with him too, because I have done a lot of joint work with him in the personality disorder service.

I often see my CPN with her child when she pops by the Links Café on a weekend; we natter and then go our separate ways.

And lastly, my MHO. She is a very good friend of one of my best friends. She's new and I haven't learnt how to talk to her yet. I think she is puzzled because she can't see anything much wrong with me. She has done all sorts of things to sort out various problems and had long conversations with my named person. She's been part of training events where we have lectured on detention. Maybe it is awkward for her.

She's another person I would like to walk along the beach with. It feels like you need to get to know the people who are doing these things to you before you can speak to them openly.

Between them, I know these different people have and do keep me alive. Not only have they kept me alive, they have given me the support that allows me to do a stressful job, to recover from the various sad things I need to recover from and to begin to build a life and a set of friends who also keep me alive and thrilled to see the sun and the sea.

Oh, and I do know I play a part in that too, in case you are leaping around saying, 'Stop being so passive, so dependant, so uncritical.'

Many people say I should hate such people. I don't know why I should hate people who have given me the chance to find my life again. The only reason I could be angry is that I know I owe a debt of obligation that their profession, and their way of being, does not allow them to acknowledge and will not allow me to discharge.

April

UNDERAGE SINGING

You only arrived a few hours ago and somehow I have arranged for us to go to a concert that Helen's sons are giving. The second punk concert in my life, except the oldest musician is fourteen and the youngest eleven and it is being held in a village hall in the middle of nowhere.

You are amenable. Let's say slightly bemused, but amenable.

Just as we are about to leave the house, I see a familiar sight walking down the road towards me. Harry has come to visit with his rucksack and his knitting. I wonder where he has been today? He lives down in Edinburgh but I first met him when he lived in Caithness. He goes on journeys, never telling people he is on his way, just relying on the warmth of friends and strangers to find somewhere to sleep the night.

He has a story he tells about disability and how it is 'a fucking pain', about his brain operations, his mental illness and learning disability but most of all about his friendly squares that he knits all the time, with the ambition of giving away as many squares as possible, as a symbol of love and peace, to everyone he meets. This is even though he hates knitting, but because he is a man and men don't knit, he therefore has to knit. And he is a lovely, lovely person; someone it is an honour to know but difficult to know what to do with, when you are just setting out to watch a young person's punk band play in the village hall.

I'm not sure why he is here this time as usually he visits me on my birthday (he keeps a list of hundreds of birthdays in a battered notebook in his pocket.)

Either way, Harry, you and me reach the hall to be met with hugs from Helen and slight confusion from lots of people I don't know.

I like that the days are like this when you are here; that things happen. That nothing is certain and that almost anything might occur before the day is finished.

THE BACK OF THE PLAYGROUND

I work with wonderful people; vibrant, loving, warm reflective people. People who I love to be around, love to speak with, solve the world's problems with. People who, day after day, wake up looking for hope, looking to give, looking to contribute, be valid, be normal, be as wonderful as they would love to believe they could dare to hope to be.

And yet these wonderful people often have that wee edge to them, that almost indiscernible tremor of hurt. I have never seen anyone with blank eyes but I hear stories that make me sad that this world is the way it is. I think it is sad that the world is so.

I hate the way that when you are sad that people avoid you: catch sight of you and cross the street so that they don't have to talk to you. I hate the way that when loneliness is the only thing you have to wrap around yourself at night, that people see you sitting alone and ask if they can take the chairs from your table and leave you with your solitary pint or glass of wine.

I hate that as the night passes, the beer loses its taste and the book you took with you has paragraphs you read over again and again until you open the door out of the pub, out into the dark misty world and walk slow steps home, having said nothing to anyone.

But most of all I hate those self-satisfied people who say the route to a good, balanced, happy life is to surround yourself with good, balanced, happy people. Those complacent, arrogant people, probably *Guardian* readers and *Independent* readers who say, 'Take the toxic people out of your life, surround yourself with those people who can bring you joy.

And I think, *What about us? The toxic people, the lonely people?*

The people who walk, looking at the ground. The people you recognise but pass by in the street. What about us? The people who crave a hug at least once or twice a year. The people who are so desperate for a conversation or for love, or for some form of faint recognition that the moment we end up on the edge of your circles we make fools of ourselves, fasten that lonely, set apart cloak more and more firmly around ourselves.

What about us? Who at school sat at the back of the class and never spoke, who walked at the edge of the playground, who got teased because we were so fat or who got talked about because we were so thin and so silent. The wee rejects who watched as you all lived lives of scintillating drama, full of passion and emotion, lives where you all talked to each other on the phone in the evening. We were not a part of it; we sat alone at home, staring at the television. You, who studied literature or art, who starred on the stage or danced at parties; you, who became excited little politicians seeking out social justice for the dispossessed and the downtrodden, but careful to avoid us, who silently walked the corridors of the schools where we had nothing to do and no one to talk to.

And now in adulthood, with collections of unremarkable memories, where our conversation pieces are so insignificant we don't even bother to tell them, we watch you in the pubs, with your children, being successful, walking your dogs, holding parties. We read about people like you in the papers.

When we sit alone in cafes, we see you with your friends. When we lie in bed we hear you walking home from the pub in the dark, laughing, and we twist our hands that wee bit because we know we would not shine if you chapped at our door and said, 'Come away out to party with us.'

We would not brighten if you stopped us in the street and tried to talk to us. Your children would not burst with their smiles if you asked us into your house.

I hate the way that those people who laugh and run, and look at people with welcome and joy, do attract other people who laugh and run and look at people with welcome and joy, and that many of the people I know are like the cartoon characters who walk the streets and look in the windows and know those happy faces are not for them.

That to dare to hope for that is to have hope way above your station.

I hate that, because the happy people attract other happy people that they are likely to stay happy, even when they bounce from drama to drama, while the lonely people don't even attract other lonely people. Because if you're lonely and sad it is usually the happy people you want, not the sad people.

It sucks. It makes you angry. It's how it is. I do this too. I rage against this injustice, this cruelty that is the way the world operates, that says the runt will be pushed further and further from the milk until it becomes too weak to try any longer. That says that the poorly chicken will be pecked at by the other chickens until it is too frail to stand up for itself. That is the bewildering picture of a child being pushed from group to group in a playground by its laughing peers because it doesn't understand, hasn't learnt the rules of how to belong, when all it wants is that sense of belonging.

And I do it because, although my work is that constant battle for a voice for that child in the playground, who is now an adult wondering just what proportion of his life he can devote to telly, I find I gravitate to the sparky, the vibrant too. I am just as much a hypocrite.

I love the people who bubble and sparkle. I love silliness and laughter. I glow when I am around such people, and when I am in the company of people who obviously wish to speak but cannot think of anything interesting to say, I see myself fidgeting, becoming tongue-tied.

I say to myself that I need to lighten their day, and scowl at how inept I am at the social skills needed to bring a wee touch of joy to the set-apart.

I look for excuses to come off the phone, or to leave the room, to do something else. And I remember my friend who giggles and jokes and tells me that she far prefers schizophrenics like me to the depressives she meets. She seems to think we have a bit of spark, that we haven't given up. That we are confident in the outrageousness of our unreality. And although I know it is untrue and that I am way up there in the stakes of how to be boring, I preen, feel that shiver of satisfaction that says maybe my life is at least a bit interesting, maybe my conversation is not always too dull to concentrate on.

*

I think back to many, many years ago, when I was young and naïve and impressionable and working on a kibbutz on the Lebanese border in Israel. I remember, and will always remember and bore person after person with the story of the old man with the eye patch, the old, thin but still fit man. The one with the lines on his face and such a strict voice, but very few sentences.

I remember how he liked me very much and would not let me be rotated into other areas of kibbutz work. I remember we were told that he spent his childhood in the early years of the war, locked in a cupboard, stuck in the dark until the Nazis found him and took him away, away to Auschwitz, with its darkly smoking chimneys. The place where his wrist was tattooed and hundreds and hundreds of thousands of people were slaughtered. The place I read about in books with a fascinated horror, a sick curiosity, wanting to see those awful images.

And when he was liberated, he found himself in Israel, on the kibbutz with a wife and a son. And his son grew into an adult and went to fight in one of Israel's wars and was killed. And his wife was consumed with grief and took to obliterating that grief, that horror, with the sweet, sharp, darkness of alcohol until, over the years it caught up with her, wrapped itself around her liver and her blood until she too faded and died.

I think to myself of him and how he lived, and still lived with pride and dignity, and how I came to think that the minor bangs and upsets of childhood, the wee sets of tears and spells of sadness and loneliness and dislocation do not mount up to one, one hundred millionth of what he went through.

I think to myself that I demean the people around me and shame myself if I try to explain my life with tales of trauma. That when I talk of trauma it is like dancing through meadows with butterflies compared to what so many people I know have been through.

And I know. Because I tell people too; the savage burn of experience is not constant, or otherwise no Jew from the thirties, no black man from

89

South Africa in the fifties, no survivor of famine and no refugee from conflicts I have never heard of would be free of torment and illness.

And those who gasp blank-eyed and say, "It hurt when you looked at me in that way, it hurt when I feared you had left me, it hurt when I put my hand up in class and everyone laughed."

And who, still today, cringe at the statements that let them know they are not perfect and I know, I know so well that these realities too contain their own dark seeds, and those dark seeds have their own parasites that feed so blindly on our inner faith but, even though I know, I turn to myself and say, 'I never suffered, not in that way, so why, when I look over my shoulder, do I wince and say "I wish, I wish it had been different?"'

That edge I talk of, that hurt. Maybe I talk of something we all have, but when I think of it, I think of people who have been marked in some way, maybe by the pain of the past, or even the pain of the future but more by that sense of apartness. Most of all I think of those people I know, who live for the time that they may be acknowledged and loved.

I think of the outbursts when we are trying to discuss issues, that raw energy which silences and sometimes makes us angry because we may have similar tales we do not want to impose on ourselves or others.

The sudden gushing in a discussion on care homes being overtaken by the experience of being a young child, mute, alone in a slaughterhouse full of maggots, waiting for the feared caress.

I think of the casual laughing conversations about being beaten up by husbands, of knowing what it is like to have your bones broken by someone who says he loves you.

I think of the odd line in my thoughts when someone says they were sorry they couldn't come to the meeting because they were in hospital after another overdose, or meeting with social workers to see when they could see their children again, or they are off to see if they can get their benefits reinstated or they would like to help our cause, but first they need to find somewhere they can live and sleep out of the rain.

It is that apartness, the fact that we can, and do, casually litter our conversation with tragedy without realising that many people cannot hear what we say and do not want to hear it. It is almost the fact that we become conversation pieces, that our darkest moments, the things that make us separate are the sorts of things people like me put on a page like this.

It is that I can write that my good friend's house smelt of burnt meat for days after her dad had a heart attack and fell into the fire when she was a child; that she went to school as normal on the day of his funeral and came back to find the gathering of relatives after the burial, in progress. That she didn't have anyone to explain to her what had happened when her mum was taken away after attempting suicide, that her brother was killed in a car crash and when I sit late at night and hear stories such as these, I understand why she may sometimes talk incessantly, never pausing or relaxing till she slips into those days when the world is a grey cotton with dark clouds.

It is that edge, the wee quirks, the people who smile vaguely and never speak much, but whose hands are covered in cigarette burns, who shyly hand in small articles for newsletters in which they say when they harm themselves they are remembering the fists of their father.

It is that edge where someone absents herself after too long in our company, needing space, needing not to think.

It is the person who cannot decide whether to show the deep twisted scars that litter and distort her wrist or by not showing them admit to shame, who has to say to strangers, 'Oh, don't hug me, I can't do hugs.'

Or the person who will not eat food in public, has to politely refuse every offer of meat or cheese or bread when around others at lunchtime.

I remember years ago, Mark would start dancing with someone in a nightclub and say, 'Hi I'm Mark, I'm manic depressive.'

And sometimes that was a good thing to say.

I don't understand those layers of judgement with which we cloak our interactions and beliefs about each other. Those half-bitten words that say, 'You, the mentally ill, are really failures, are really the losers, the frauds, the scroungers.'

That say with slight changes in expressions, and through small, easily retracted innuendoes, that,

'Although we do not judge, we do know that if only you did do the pulling together, move beyond the helpless self-pity, start to employ just a scrap of logic to your reasoning and a modicum of sense to your arguments and a levelling of order in your emotions. If you did this, as everyone can. If you just put a bit of effort into it, then life would be easy, would be fine and dandy and we could all just get on with the day to day job of living.'

It makes me furious that there is this attitude. I am furious at the lack of compassion and understanding. At the complete ignorance this all betrays, as if mental illness is a simple puzzle to solve, just tweak here, add some hope, a bit of friendship, a job or two and there you go.

And I am furious because I believe it too.

I look at some of my friends and companions when they are slack with a despair so profound it doesn't even have the energy to call itself despair. And I want to grab my friends by the shoulders and shake them back and forward so their hair flies in all directions and slowly a spark of something appears in their eyes. I want to shake them and say, 'Stop it! Stop this helpless, hopeless mess you are in. Stop this apathy, this slow, slow descent into oblivion.'

I want to shake them back into life, back into being the vibrant, loving people I know them to be and I cannot, and I know I will not and that it would never work, but I want to so much.

And I am furious because I listen to these comments. Sometimes I think to myself, *I am also severely or long-termedly or enduringly ill, according to the people around me, and yet I work. I work really, really, really hard. I take responsibility for myself, my organisation and other people.* I think, *Would it really be impossible for you to work in a shop or a factory? Is it really that hard to earn a wage, the way so many other people do with so many other problems in their life?*

And as I think of this, I probe into my heart and I shout into it, 'Graham, listen to yourself! Do you not remember those years on the dole, those years where night was day, where food was an afterthought, and too expensive anyway. Surely you remember that work was beyond you? Was incomprehensible? Surely you remember that there was a time when you were not signed off sick but you were not working. When getting up was an achievement and walking to the pub an achievement. It wasn't a question of can't or won't work, it was plain old impossible!'

And as I think this, I remember those hectoring letters from my mother, telling me over and over to get on my feet, to get together, to stop relying on the state, to stop this inadequacy, this scrounging weakness and I remember how incoherently angry this made me feel.

I am furious because the thoughts worm themselves inside us like bilharzia. Little worms eating away at us, taking away our vision, making us think,

Maybe it's true. Maybe if I just got on with it. Maybe I am weak, maybe I am a failure, maybe I will never be successful or attractive or admired or loved.

Maybe, if we take away the word mental illness, we see a collection of inadequate, miserable, shy, argumentative people; we see people who are particularly good at gathering the qualities the rest of the world rejects and avoids, and in this smear we can erect whole castles of unhappiness. We can say,

'Yes you are right. I am pathetic and my illness is a pretence, and my need for assistance so ridiculous that I will stop seeking help, stop trying at all.'

We build this negativity up so high that the worms eat right through us until there is nothing left, just this knowledge that we deserve nothing, should have nothing; are no use because we are mentally ill.

We take on the judgement of our society and judge ourselves far harsher and for far longer and with much more effect than we knew we were capable of.

SPRING AT THE RIVER

I take a leaf, I pluck it from the ground. I suppose I should think of the destruction that causes. Wee tendrils, wee veins (but in plant language) poke out of the split stem.

I hold the leaf to my mouth. It smells green, that green, green, cool, fresh smell, that scent of spring. I brush the leaf over your face and you smile and reach up and hold my hand.

I lie down on the grass, scrunch the leaf up. It splits, it goes dark, dark green in the creases. It is like tired cardboard, all furry and floppy. I throw it away and it falls beyond sight, down the bank of a stream where the dock leaves and the nettles live.

I grip a stem of grass and tug softly; it slips out of the sheath of its home to reveal a thin white delicate stem that has never seen the light before. I nibble on the end, sucking the sweetness out until the flavour has gone and the grass is flat and soggy.

I pick two more pieces of grass. We lie on our backs, giggling in a muffled way, chewing on the grass, feeling the sunshine on our faces. We spit the soggy ends out. Mine falls off my chin onto my shirt and stains it green. I pluck it off, toss it away and lean over to give you a kiss before we get up and walk along the river, under the green trees with the smooth water and the darting birds, our hands entwined, our hips knocking against each other.

DAY TO DAY

Hmm, three years of being detained. What have I done in that time? Let's see. A typical day.

A typical day. I don't suppose there is a typical day for anyone. I wake. Sometimes I wake very early indeed and turn on the radio because I do not like the silence of my bed, and sometimes I doze and listen to the seagulls outside the window and the sound of cars beginning to make the morning more real. Getting out of bed can be difficult, it sort of depends on my mood and how much whisky I drank the night before.

When I get to the sitting room I'm always frustrated at my curtains that sort of get jammed when I try to open them and then it is time to wait for the coffee to flow up into its wee container.

Everything has its time and place. While the coffee is on the stove, I tidy away the dishes from the night before, hanging up the pots on their rack and the knives on their magnetic bar, putting the plates in the cupboard. I might decide to have toast but it depends on how palatable food seems in the morning to me.

Once the coffee is ready I lie on the couch with my mug on the table beside me and for a few moments I might read or listen to Radio 4. Then, when the clock hand reaches the right minute, I set off for work.

I drive for half an hour to Inverness, listening to Radio 1 or Moray Firth Radio, and work varies. It always seems very intense, very busy, very consuming. Sometimes I am in the office doing 'stuff': having meetings, writing emails and letters and making phone calls. At other times I am somewhere in the Highlands; off to meet people, discuss things. I may be pottering off to Skye or Ullapool, up to Wick or down to Lochaber. I am so used to the journeys now that I pay them little attention, but it may be that I see a mountain lit up by the morning sun with snow on its summit or I might yet again wonder why I don't pause to drink coffee by a still loch or walk on a sunny beach. Sometimes I do, but not often.

It is strange sometimes to be rushing round the Highlands, busy talking about changing the world and then driving into the golden sun and the half shadows lighting up a mountainside or illuminating the sea, or driving round a corner and seeing yachts or small ships nuzzled into moorings; driving along and pausing with a foot on a shuddering brake as one then another deer runs out on the road in front of you while at the same time talking of illness and despair and the mechanics of the ways out of despair.

When I reach where I am going, I am always welcomed. After all these years I know most people I go to see quite well. It makes conversation and discussion much easier. I meet wonderful people, full of talent and warmth and yet so often denied the opportunity to make a difference or to do anything much at all. Between us we speak out and dream and believe in something, and somehow I get paid to do that while they tend not to be. Somehow, we preach openness and trust and acceptance, using all those skills and talents and strengths that we sometimes forget we ever had, that we somehow misplaced. And we look out for each other, believe in each other. It is a good life; a good job to do.

If I am setting off south then I tend to arrive at the station early and look for a spare unreserved table to work at. Often it is dark when I get on the train and dark on my return journey too, but even when it isn't, I generally hunch over my laptop, taking advantage of the time when no one will disturb me, catching up on my work. And the mountains will flicker past; the herds of deer and flocks of sheep swish past and it will be a rare day that I or my fellow passengers pause to take them in.

Some days I work at home. I sit on my bed with my laptop and coffee and music. The coffee never gets drunk and the music isn't heard and I will get lost in whatever it is that I am typing. Evenings, I do little. Sometimes, if I am enthusiastic, I go for a walk to the beach or the harbour, sometimes I babysit, sometimes I visit people, often I am late home from work. But when I am home it is usually whisky and food and t.v. and bed as soon as I can let myself do so without feeling too much shame at my early nights.

That's sort of my routine. Every two weeks I get my jag, I see my CPN or psychiatrist and still have thoughts and knowledge I do not want. Often I look in my bathroom cabinet at the pack of razor blades and wish I had the courage to use them and yes, I am lost and empty. I can be that grey ash self I try to ignore, and I can be very lonely and crave someone to talk to properly, crave someone to hold and be held by. I do struggle to talk, even at the best of times. Oh, I can perform at work and when it is clear what to say, but when I am sitting, dredging my mind for conversation, I just get so lost, there is so often nothing there; like I peer into some treasure chest of stories and find they have all been used up, gone mouldy, so mouldy that I can't even drag them out for my friends or my family. Often I drown out the world with alcohol, but I get through the days and sometimes I enjoy them very much, feel fulfilled and energised by what I do. It's a pretty ordinary life. Unremarkable in a way, although being me, I want to remark on it every day.

MIST

Somehow, mist has it all. I think of mist in the rainforest, twining itself around the trees and leaving a shine on their leaves. I think of the mist rising from the ground, the warm hot ground where the leeches live and the insects and birds shrill and then, there it is, stretching out above the forest canopy in tendrils, looking silent, looking still and exotic.

And I think of mist on a hill in Scotland. Of red, raw hands and water dripping from chins and noses, of sudden swirls of wind that blow holes in the whiteness and reveal black cliffs and the lochs far down below; a path meandering along the edge of precipices. Of course, the sound of crows and ravens and the slight shudder of cold, the threat of a hint of misery at this slippery path, with shiny grey stones and lichen. The tap of boots making the silence even more deafening.

I think of mist or fog at sea, the slow slip of the boat in almost no wind, the oily lap of the waves and far off, the sound of fog horns. The wooden decks covered in moisture, the water droplets falling from the sails, slipping off the boom. And us, sitting damply with mugs of tea, staring out around us anxiously, startling when, of a sudden, we see the rapid approach of a ship out of the mist, first a grey shape, then a bow wave, then the heavy thrum of the engines and, in an instant it is away again, swallowed by the silent white fog.

And I remember last weekend, driving home. Driving home, while the sun set, all red across the clouds, all golden on the hills and then the dark came down and for mile after mile I passed the silent blink of the speed cameras and wished I was back home with you.

At Drummochter the mist was low and the headlights bounced back their own glare into my face. Approaching Dulnain Bridge, a car approaching lit up the fog hanging above the road, an orange-grey blur of something hanging and swirling just bare feet above our heads while the road below was clear and the tree trunks went past in a blur.

Finally up on the Dava moor, driving into bank after bank of fog, driving through clear spaces, seeing the stars, the heather, then picking out the line of whiteness ahead, the bright blare of mist; suddenly slowing down, feeling along, hoping no cars would drive fast in the other direction along this narrow road, hoping the deer and the sheep stay put until, all of a sudden, I am out of the fog bank, the road dips and I am back in the silence again.

At last, from the top of the moor I see the coast in the distance and feel relief, and realise that while I have been concentrating I haven't been thinking of you at all.

SETTLING THE GHOSTS
– LEAVING THE HAUNTING

I have had in my mind as I have been writing this, this part of my story, the bit where the mess begins and which sets a seal and a coffin lid on our shared memories and histories; buries something profound into the world of the victim and the oppressor, the abuser and the survivor. And yet, I find life to be more complicated than that. So much more complicated.

I hear people talk of types and categories of people; of the unforgivable and the forgivable, of the irredeemable, and the politics of power and gender and control and this whole mountain that we pile on ourselves. This mountain that makes change impossible, that makes reconciliation something we feel guilty about, that makes guilt something we feel guilty about.

I hate the tight morality that binds us into such rigidity of good and bad, the victim and the villain.

Because I will. I do not know why, but I will reduce my wife to a stereotype, the person that people will say of, 'How could she do that? How did he put up with this?' Or maybe I won't, maybe people will say, 'What a pathetic self-justifying man.'

And I will plead with you to read the next page where I give the lie to that. Because in the years that have passed, I have made a history; a story of my life, my adulthood and I have cast myself in the role of the survivor of the debris and yes, I am a survivor, but I think the debris is imaginary.

Life had always been delightful with her, until the day that my wife insisted I tell her who I fancied apart from her. Went on and on, when we were lying cuddled in bed, warm with our love. On and on until I thought of someone I thought was attractive and said her name.

I am so naïve. I did not know you are not meant to find other people attractive when you are in love, and to be honest it was only the vaguest attraction, but I was trying to give her an answer that I thought she wanted. I can't believe I was so silly.

It was our first proper argument. Well, argument is not the word. It was the first time everything went wrong. I remember writhing on the floor, begging her to believe that I loved her and did not love anyone else, and crying and sobbing. Her voice, hurt, going on and on. I remember the spoon or the knife or the nail clippers that were in my hand, whatever it was, bending double and gouging into me until it snapped. From then, from that day on, for the next year, once a week or so, I would be met with the accusation of what I had done by fancying someone. Sometimes I would say that I didn't fancy anyone else, that I didn't mean it, that I was just making it up. I grew desperate to escape my betrayal and the words went on and on and on and on.

I would be crying and I would not understand and I would just be so confused and lost and I just didn't know what I had done wrong. I didn't understand why she didn't believe I loved her.

In the pub she would catch me looking at a woman and get cross and say that I had a roving eye, a wandering eye; and a part of me thought, *Surely that comes from the fifties? Surely no one talks of the roving eye anymore?*

I would wonder who I had been looking at and how I had been looking at them, and I would try not to look at women when I went to the pub.

I did not understand the arguments that grew over the years. They would catch me unawares. Initially I would be talking away and then I would become aware that there was a silence, that something had gone wrong, and my memory is that I would ask what I had done wrong, how I had hurt her and she would say if I didn't know then it was even worse.

After the raised voices there would be that silence, those tight lips. I would be angry, and hurt and confused and usually drunk by then. Over the hours I would beg to be told how I had hurt her and eventually I would be told and we would go round in circles. I would deny it and then I would seek to find out in my heart what I might have done, how I might have hurt her without meaning to and I would see how I might have, that maybe she was right and so I would reach out to apologise and ask for forgiveness.

And she would ignore me. She would ignore me until I teased her and danced around her and begged her and eventually I would make her laugh; then she would tell me that I was a bastard and smile and say I wasn't forgiven, but we would have a hug and I would relax.

In the twenty years of arguments the only time that she ever admitted she was ever in the wrong was in the twenty-fourth year of our partnership.

The first time she threw a glassful of wine in my face, I forget when, it would be sometime before our son was born. I couldn't believe it. Surely this only happened in movies? It didn't sting. I was just very wet and my shirt stuck to me. My lips and my eyes and my nose were wet and cold and I was a wee bit stunned.

Eventually this became routine: an argument, I will have a drink thrown at me, I will be that bit less surprised than last time. I have lost count of the number of times she finished arguments this way and walked out of the room.

The arguments were so bad. It was like you were in a whirlwind of shards of glass shredding you, slicing you smaller and smaller until there was nothing left, until you were desperate, just wanted the words to stop, to stop hearing how awful and pathetic you were.

Sometimes, well, on three occasions in a couple of months, not very long after my son was born, the words overwhelmed me and I pinned her to the bed and I shouted at her to stop shouting at me, to stop speaking to me, to be quiet. And she would be quiet.

Then she told me how frightened she felt when I did that and I understood what I was doing and never did anything like it again, until seventeen years later when it all went wrong, finally. And then too, there is that litany, that tired, tired litany that is so common and banal. After my son was born we lost the intimacy that comes from being a couple. It went away. We moved from Edinburgh and the romance of being a couple shut down.

I didn't understand. I thought if I cuddled her, kissed her, caressed her, she would feel loved. She said that I worked so hard and drank so much that she felt unloved, that she felt no desire for me, that she didn't feel love for me. That I was a stranger to her.

Life became such that if I cuddled her in the kitchen she would tell me to stop molesting her. If we went to bed she would turn her back to me. If she got undressed she would insist I didn't look at her.

Eventually a year went by when she would get undressed and into her nightgown, all the while keeping her outer clothes on, and then she would get into bed without looking at me and ask me to turn out the light and not to read my book. I felt like a pervert.

I felt jealous on the beach, on holiday, when she went topless and I and everyone else would see more of her body in those brief days than I had seen in the entire previous year. I felt lonely. I felt incompetent. I felt helpless.

I did not know what to do. I thought to express love physically was to demonstrate that wonder and joy you have in each other. She found she had lost that wonder and could only regain it if I showed her love in the way she needed it. In the intimacy of our thoughts and our valuing of each other. And neither of us could bridge our apartness. So we grew apart.

I found, more and more, that those attempts to talk and to confide escaped us. We wounded each other when we tried to talk to each other. I found that my hopes that I could look after her, that I could listen to her feelings, were inadequate and I think that was because the feelings of unhappiness she had were all to do with me. I think this was because she felt she did all the looking after, made all the decisions and felt alone with them.

As my son grew up he would compete for attention and status. Often, when we walked along the pavement he would walk beside her and I would walk behind. As he grew older, if she was driving he would insist on sitting in the front of the car with her, with me in the back, and I would feel humiliated and angry, and powerless and insignificant. She would tell me to stop overreacting and I would think to myself that maybe she was right, that I was being trivial. And the arguments they just went on and on.

Sometimes there were evenings of arguments where the subject of the argument was not what we were arguing about. Often the arguments arose out of a friendly conversation, a joyful dinner and suddenly we were in an argument and I didn't know what I had done, where it had come from. I didn't know. I didn't know.

There were months (or was it years?) when I banished myself to another room. As I became fat, I began to snore; I found that I preferred my tiny room with its single bed and minute window to the coldness of a bed where I felt unwanted.

I spent months waiting for them to finish watching telly in the upstairs sitting room so I could go to bed in the box room adjoining it. I hated that.

I hated being alone but sometimes I found a sense of joy in it. To be alone and free of that turned back was a release sometimes.

I still find it hard to believe that I was told I was too boring for us to invite friends round. I remember that conversation so clearly. I remember my hurt and my incomprehension and my feeling that it must be true but somehow it was all so wrong.

I wasn't allowed to invite my friends home because they had mental health problems and were too connected to my work, and I wasn't allowed to make friends who had mental health problems. When, on rare occasions, people did visit, the house would go into a panic; a panic of tidying and getting ready and usually everything would be fine, it would be joyous. But sometimes it wasn't and my wife would talk and laugh and be charming and then, when they were gone, whisper furiously to me when we were in bed and turn her back on me again.

We kept my illness a secret from the people in the village. I was not allowed to be public about it, in the way I wanted, for fear of the reaction, the dread fear of what might be said and what might happen to my son if everyone knew his dad had schizophrenia. I found it hard that I couldn't be public about my life when my whole job was about taking away that particular shame.

As time went by I would write Christmas letters, and I am a person who does not know secrecy, as you can see in this story. I loved the Christmas letters. People would write back and say how they hated all 'round robin' Christmas letters except the one I sent, and I was so proud. But as the years went by and life became darker, they would be edited more and more by my wife, hints and words of unhappiness or conflict began to be removed. I would have to show them to her and agree the changes she wanted made and the Christmas letters that people said were delightful, because they were open and trusting and frank, became letters of charm, divorced from reality, containing a reality that, by its hints at sadness, disguised a far deeper and darker sadness.

I started writing, and being me, I often wrote of my life and my landscape and these pieces of writing also had to be submitted to my wife for approval. I railed against this because I wanted to write as I thought, to write what I felt and what I wanted to express.

Then, when, inexcusably, I began to confide my loss and my unhappiness to Sarah and my wife became aware that I liked her very much, I would get angry text after angry text when I was away and I would be expected to phone every day, but there would be pauses on the phone and silences and my stomach would coil at the silence. After a time my phone would be taken and monitored for the texts I sent. Eventually I was forbidden to mention my wife's name or my son's name, or anything about my family when I went to work and I was forbidden to work away from home with Sarah. I was told if we were in the car we were not to sit side by side,.That one should sit in the front and one in the back and that conversation should be only about work, nothing at all about anything else and I railed about this too. I couldn't understand why I wasn't allowed to talk about my family to anyone, especially as Sarah seemed to give me such good advice, seemed to have such good ideas for making things better.

They were terrible, terrible times. Being in hospital is awful but those evenings, dreading the ring of the phone, feeling sick when it rang, sick at what would be said, what would be said about me, sick that when I went silent I was told off and when I argued I was told off. People in the corridor would hear me, would hear the pain of those calls and I would be begging to be let go, to be let go, and yet I couldn't escape.

Oh, I can feel in my stomach those silences on the phone, while my nurse sat watch at the door, like my heart was being burnt away and somehow I was responsible for it.

Food is my gift to everyone. It's what I do as a way of contributing. Offering something, even if it is not much. My wife got fed up with my food, asked me to stop going to such an effort, to stop the lavishness of the meals. Sometimes, on bad days, orange juice would be thrown over the just-prepared meal.

On another occasion the dining table was turned on its side and all the food and crockery fell to the floor. Or more routinely, we'd argue and a full plate of food would be immediately scraped into the bin.

I don't know why I revisit these times, these memories, these sadnesses of what we did to each other.

I remember my sister visiting just after Christmas, one of her rare, once every three year visits, and my wife offered to babysit so we could all go out, but we were late back. Maybe two hours later than we said we would be. She was polite when we returned, but I was made to sleep on the floor at the foot of the bed. She got fed up with me being there and made me sleep on the floor in the sitting room, calling me back to the bedroom floor before anyone else got up. Then she went out, and I didn't know what to say to my sister. So I think I didn't say anything.

She came back just before my sister left to go south again and then left with my son to go to a party that we had all been invited to, telling me to stay behind. And at this I called Sarah up and asked to stay at hers because I was leaving. Another stupid thing to do.

I was a wee bit obsessed, a wee bit wishing she, Sarah, would hug my sorrow away. That was the first time I left.

I lasted a day until the suicide threats became too much and I came back. Back to something I no longer remember and cannot describe. Not trauma. I just don't remember. Back to attempts to solve what we were going through. Attempts that were years too late.

It was so late, so completely beyond any point at which we could make amends, could forgive, could relearn the elements of the love that had permeated our lives for so many years. That love which at one time we took for granted and yet somehow, and I don't really know how, disappeared.

When I try to think about it, I feel this lump in my throat that is both a welling of tears, a surge of anger and a tired lament of despair. I do not know if it started when love began to seep out of our lives or if it was some dynamic; some way of relating and acting that was embedded from the start in our relationship.

I know I lived on tenterhooks and I know that I wanted to please and yet I couldn't please. And I know that a basic deficit in my heart is that of the sense of worth that most people have to some extent. I can see how wearying it can be when, because a person has no confidence and little dynamism, that their partner finds they are somehow in charge. Somehow they are, in a confused way, the person you defer to, pander to, and I can see how that must be so terribly, terribly wearying: that constant responsibility. But from my point of view there was also the resentment at not having a valid point of view, of being so used to messing things up, that always I felt a tension, a *Will I get this wrong? And will I have the first idea of what I have done wrong?* And that unutterable pit of fear and worry in my stomach when the laughter turns sour and the consequences of your failings become apparent; not for the next hour, but for the evening, the night, the next day, maybe the day after that. Until you manage to humble yourself, humiliate yourself in search of a smile and a kind word.

When it was obvious to both of us that our marriage was lost, or at least in the midst of a storm, with flapping sails and breaking masts, and lots of shouting that does not make sense in the shrieking wind and the heavy brutal waves. At this point it became something vicious. I will not list the things that my wife did to me, but they caused my heart to both harden and be filled with anxiety and a terrible, terrible pain. And so yes, it was far too late. In the midst of foundering, we tried to clean the decks and coil the ropes, when, all the while, the dark sea was seeking us.

Those years. Oh, I shudder to remember them and I know, in many ways, I was responsible. I had drawn away, I had refused to accept my unstated role anymore and the consequences were dire. I saw this as an attempt to stand up for myself, to gain an identity and a sense of independence but it turned out to be threatening and so devastating to both of us. I believe, though I may be wrong, that the reason I last went into hospital after I had left my wife, was partly because of the gut-wrenching anxiety of our separation, the grief of the loss of my son and the grief that that circle of people who I had shared the last twenty years with had just vanished. And finally, but most importantly, it was the silences I keep mentioning. It was those phone calls where silence carried on for minutes and you could just feel loathing and contempt driving down the phone lines and I would get more and more frantic and hollow in my stomach. Those sudden emails where I would feel physically sick when I saw the email address, even before actually looking at them. Those letters when my hands would tremble as I opened the envelope and on reading would feel shattered, as though I had become pale, see-through; a ghost of what I had hoped to be. And the silent evenings, alone and lonely.

I remember Sarah tried to find some way of gaining control of my finances and my decision-making powers at one point. She felt that I was not acting rationally; that the burden of separation, the guilt of leaving, my illness as people saw it; the whole awfulness of it all, meant that I was putting myself at risk and indeed, making decisions that would ultimately damage me hugely. And she was right. So right. I may not have been acting out of illness but the pain of it all, the interminable pain and the constant fear that I would not be free of it meant that I lost so many of our joint assets as to beggar belief in the reality of sense and fairness and justice. I wish Sarah had succeeded in gaining control of my finances. It would have ruined my relationship with her and it is true that for many years we had the most wonderful of friendships where much of what she did in my life kept me sane and hopeful, and so ultimately it would have been a disaster if she had become some legal guardian of my life, but it might have stopped some of the decisions I was making willy-nilly, in an attempt to stop the pain and the guilt from consuming me.

It was at the point when everything had fallen apart that I knew one or other of us would be killed if I stayed, and that the psychiatrist who had warned me my life was in danger had not done so lightly. It was at that point, that moment of shame, when everything had finally collapsed around us and no, I will not say exactly what happened except that I knew I had to leave. And so, some weeks later, after almost a phony war of not much being said, despite hostilities being declared, I did. First I went to the house of a work colleague and I remember that clearly, but not the order of things. I remember the brightness of my friend and her husband, I remember the room I slept in but most of all I remember this sort of limbo, a sort of *this isn't happening, I haven't really left* and yet knowing finally I had, almost like that lump you have been telling yourself is a part of your imagination is now, in fact, fatal. And despite this, I went back. Later I heard that a friend of Sarah's had a spare flat with a cheap rent in Nairn and so I left again.

That flat was a wonderful refuge: a place to talk and sleep and drown my sorrows. I remember new friends, new acquaintances, meals and walks and trips to cafes and the sun, the sun. I remember it as a sunny time but I remember it also as the sort of sunny time when you are so dehydrated that you are trembling, parched, about to go into shock and yet are unaware that it is the lack of water and the heat that is contributing to the way you are feeling. After all those years there was no other way it could be, there was no other outcome to the break with my wife and also my son, though I hadn't known I was leaving him, other than a search for death. And yet I was held so tenderly in the hearts of the people I got to know in Nairn that they made the final collapse of my marriage that bit softer, the loneliness and darkness such that there was often a tinge of the blush of dawn to my memories of even the most solitary and harsh nights.

Now I live alone. The possessions I left with were the leftovers: the knackered car, the cds we had put out for the charity shop, the Ikea table from the shed, some books. The photographs that were of me. That is the history I tell myself of my life. And which I tell some of the people I am close to, if I am especially maudlin. I find it hard to look at otherwise.

I feel as though all those years together have been erased, that I have no right to them. I meet so many people who have left relationships, who feel the need to turn their spouse into a bad person, into an ogre, and maybe that is what I am doing now.

This is where it all goes wrong. My wife was lovely. I don't know what she is like now, but she was funny and articulate. She was warm. She loved the world and the outdoors. Often, she would sing ridiculous songs; our son was the centre of her life. She believed in the environment and in justice, and in the children she worked with. She was into yoga and the Alexander technique and all sorts of things that helped her with her sense of herself and her body. She was closer to being a vegan than a vegetarian. She was just so present with everything, so engaged, so ready with smiles and laughter. And she loved me.

Often, when I explain us to me, I think we were never able to grow up together, to share our anxieties and vulnerabilities, and fears and weaknesses and so, instead of tending to each other, we turned each other into the cause of our misery.

Sometimes I ache for someone to talk to who remembers the times we spent in those decades, who could reminisce, but the people I know now knew our life so little that there is little to share. Little to chew and joke and smile about. There is no room to share those stories because no one can chime in and say, 'I remember that! Do you remember when he did that?'

No one to remember the time of the wriggle crabs on Isle de Reay, when the sun shone every day and we ate peaches and croissants and sat outside our tent in the warm evenings. The times of the magic stones at Uath Lochans. The nights we stared gobsmacked at the Northern Lights. The numerous walks round Loch an Eilein. Being with all of her wonderful family: her sisters and their partners, their children, her mum and dad. Sitting on the Braid Hills with friends and prosecco when the Millenium came round. When she taught me to ski and to drive. When

110

she gave me that confidence I was lacking, gave me a reason to smile and to look forward to the dawn, and to put aside the terrible weight of my need to harm myself. When we were both so thin we could fit easily together in a single bed.

All these stories; these years and years of wonderful stories, and I don't know how to share them. I don't know who to turn to, to say, 'Do you remember that?'

or

'She thought that and did that.'

No. Those years are now made up. They are a story that I do not know how to tell, because I do not know what is true and what is false.

I must have been horrible, always talking about work, always drinking, demonstrating love in ways that weren't appreciated. Being boring and tired, and no good at the socialising and so, so, dependent on her. And of course, going into hospital, living with whatever all this is.

May

WATER IN A SUNBEAM

It is lovely to be caught unawares by clichés and to feel that joy with which they can inspire you.

I walked into the kitchen ten minutes ago and, through the glass of the French doors, I saw a large droplet of water fall through a sunbeam. I thought of the soft rain that we have had this morning and the glimmers of brightness that break through, now that the rain has gone. I looked out at the trees, the leaves tremulous with water droplets and greenness and I felt so happy and sort of peaceful and wistful.

Somewhere there will be a haiku or some other poem about water droplets after the recent rain and I know without a doubt that if I read it, I would be pleased but I would evade whatever its message might be. I would like to say I no longer understand such things, but really I should say that I never did.

I am blind to symbolism or faith or meaning and I am not wise enough to forget this. I have a hankering to be able to say profound things and know what I am talking about, but I just reach out my hand and my mind. I see rainbows, I see the dawn and hear woodpigeons in the trees. I catch a glance between two people, I hear the most wonderful music and I am left with a vacant smile on my face or a slightly puzzled frown.

I can read to the end of a book, wracked by the words, the story, knowing that there are things contained within it that I should take away and share and muse on, but all too often, by the time I reach the end I do not remember the beginning, have no recollection of the names of the characters or the storyline, except to know that it was about love and struggles and all that messy stuff that fills our lives and keeps us talking till way after our bedtimes.

Sometimes I feel so profoundly uneducated. I could never pick up a book and realise that it is based on some other work. I could never read a chapter and think to myself about philosophy or science or art. I cannot look at a painting or a photograph and comment on it, let alone interpret it, and yet I like to read books and watch films and walk round art galleries like some water skater, gliding over the surface of a pond, making no impression on the meniscus of the water, but there, nevertheless.

My love phoned just now, off to the shops after her swim; we talked of tea, of fishcakes and whisky and going down to the station to pick her up after she gets back.

I say 'my love', and I know she is my love but I cannot really define love. I can define it by knowing that I can see her face just now, when I look inside me. I can see her blue eyes and hear her laugh; I can see her giggling, tickling me; I can hear her talking, cuddled up to me while I feel her head on my chest and her hair on my cheek. I can see her body, and as I write, I feel the touch of her lips on mine.

I can feel that delicious sense of warmth when I have comforted her and held her and organised things; I can feel the happy feeling in my tummy as I make soup downstairs while she sleeps upstairs, looking forward to her enjoyment at that first sip, hoping that I do not over oblige with little gestures like meals or tidying or chocolate; and I can feel just now how it feels when she clings to me in the kitchen when we cuddle and how I feel when I hold her tight to me in the early morning.

And I can feel me straining to be amusing and full of words, I can feel me trying to be intelligent, and I can watch me, catching glimpses of my pomposity and arrogance: trying to hide it away, trying to shove it all away, trying to live up to my vision of what I should be like to deserve such love, trying to do the looking after and to be looked after in turn.

I can hear us talking and sharing, trying out those reaches into vulnerability, trying to express those things we know so little about, trying to understand, trying to be what we dream each other had dreamed we should be.

Ah, I cannot even find a cliché! I am so ignorant at all this. Somehow I have reached my late middle age, full of naivety. I watch Wendy put on lipstick and I am filled with intrigue. I hear her talk of so many ordinary things that people do, and they are all new to me. It is like I am some long lost survivor from the forest, come into the daylight, looking all around me. Surrounded by a myriad droplets from the recent rain, all of them with their own refracted rainbows, and I want to touch each one, smooth the fresh clear water on our lips and smile and smile and smile.

A VOID IN MY HEART

I have no idea how I ended up travelling to different countries. I can't explain my adventures sailing across the Atlantic or on the South China Seas. I have no idea how I ended up climbing cliffs and easing over overhangs with the nearest bit of earth two hundred feet below me. I don't know how I skied over frozen lochs or wandered in far off deserts.

I think that, far from spontaneity, I just did what people suggested I do. I don't think I sought any of it or made any of it happen. I was just somehow there, ambling along. I have no curiosity, no interest; I don't have that spark.

I never really know what I want to do with myself. So far, I have gathered a few activities around my new life and I expect I will do them for year after year: work, telly, cooking, babysitting, charity shops, walks on the beach, occasional times with friends and that is about all there is to it. I have no ties and no obligations. I could do almost anything but I settle for routine and safety, for the comfort of the uneventful.

When I am with people I look at them, I look and think, *They are great people*, and I summon my words for a conversation and I am just like a solidified bag of wet flour.

I can just about manage, 'So what do you do?' or 'How are you?'

But then I pause, lost, wondering how to keep discussions going, how to build that bridge out of my incompetence and my passivity.

Sometimes I sit in silence and I see people, who had initially thought there might be something interesting in me, shifting uncomfortably and awkwardly wondering what to do and how to escape.

As far as I possibly can, I avoid my evil, I avoid the devil. Just like a prim aunt in the 70s would have switched channel when the sexy bits were on television. If I possibly can, I turn it off. I know it's there but I ignore it. I don't confront it or discuss it or try to understand it, I just let it be, lying there in the background, letting me know what I am really like.

But I worry. I'm good at that. I worry about everything. That's why work is good. It stops me thinking about the worrying. When I am not worrying I am trying to escape. I am reading or watching telly or cooking or trying to sleep or drinking. And that is it.

It is no wonder that I am so alone.

It is just so easy, when describing my life, to talk about all the negatives, all the sadness and yet today I feel rebellious. In my day to day life there is also a lot of laughter, there is a lot of teasing and a lot of conversation. For example, a friend just now posted on Facebook that she has a perfect life but she is sad all the time. Well, I have a wonderful life too: I do a job I love, I have friends and money and food and a place to live. I have things to do and dreams to create and it is, I suppose, just that there is that background hum that I can never avoid; that hum that pervades me, muttering about how disgusting and unutterably awful I am. I cannot block it out and so, when I come to sum up my life, it thrusts into my mind, making me forget that for much of my time I really am in buttercup fields. I am not always in the hell I think I am in.

I think it is the same when I talk of hospital. When I am a patient I am in that most awful of places; a place of horror and terror and confusion and awfulness. So when I try to tell you about what it is like in a hospital, I can confuse the abject person I am there with the reality of the stay on the ward. And of course some of it is bad, but lots and lots is very good.

I want to give you some new glimpses of my time in hospital, some of the good things. My room, for a start. The first hospital I was ever in, was a place of beds crammed together and holes in the walls and broken furniture, whilst, in contrast, the last place I was in, well! I had my own room, a bedside table and wardrobe. A walk-in shower and toilet, sockets to plug in my music and my laptop, a couple of chairs. I had a view right over Inverness, looking down the Moray Firth towards Nairn and Findhorn and Fortrose. At night, you could sit in your chair and just watch this patchwork jewellery of lights in the valley below

121

you; the dark sky, maybe the moon, twinkling lights and ships at sea. Pretty good really, pretty and peaceful and quiet. And in the daytime you could see the cloud factory near Ardersier, the Kessock bridge and the snow-covered hills, the cloud-scudded sky.

And there really was laughter at times. I think my favourite times were when the Occupational Therapist was on the ward. I remember stalking around the ward, followed all the time by my nurse, but not always that ashamed of that, and I remember I was mazy in my stomach and I was tired and light-headed from lack of food and fear, but I was also bored.

Near the nursing station, at the door, were the tables at which we were meant to eat our meals, but often in the morning these were taken over for OT stuff. At first I was too shy and awkward and plain old messed up to do anything, but, over the days, I would skirt the edge of the group doing their stuff and then I would pause in my wandering, my search for things to harm myself with, and lean on the lattice by the tables and watch, until I grew tired of refusing to join in and sat down with my fellow patients.

It can be hard to concentrate when I'm in hospital but the thing I liked doing best was squeezing this sort of liquid on patterns laid under plastic or something, which dried to make an instant sort of stained glass.

I loved it. I loved carefully applying the black lines, I loved swirling in the colour and I loved that, in a couple of hours, I would have a square that I could give to one of my friends to press onto their window. You sort of have no value as a patient, so to be able to make wee gifts for those that you love felt wonderful. But even more wonderful was how, over time, I began to speak to people. The OT person would witter away and we would join in and find ourselves talking of all those things we seemed to have lost: our families, our trips abroad, wee adventures, small stories of life melding us together, making us less separate and more connected, so that when next we sat watching the inane telly programs, we might find ourselves sitting beside someone and think to ourselves that we know the name of her children, the problems she has been having at work, her favourite walk on the Black Isle.

I have been forgetting that. I tell people about how my friend who also worked at the hospital was stopped from giving me treatment when she was seen giving me a hug, but I do not mention that before that she also gave me a hot wax foot bath that felt magic and a head massage that made me feel amazing, or that later on in my stay, she was allowed to be my escort on a walk outside the hospital; that we climbed up to Craig Dunain, walked along towards Craig Phadraig in the slight sleet and got lost. Oh! That was such fun, giggling about who would get in trouble the most for me being late back and just enjoying the wittering, the sight of the crows in the mist, the whin bushes besides the path, the vitrified fort ahead of us.

And I talk about how I was told off for trying to find ways of hanging myself when some junior nurses were on Obs with me, and how it was a harsh situation I put them in, but the nurse who told me off was my key nurse and every shift she was on, she would come into my room when she was on Obs and she would talk. Talk in such a way that I, who just couldn't talk, felt cared for and respected, felt that she wanted the best for me, wanted to know me as a person, was interested in me as that person.

There were loads of people like that. You forget, because you are clouded with the pain of memory, the everyday moments of humanity and tenderness from people there. Those times the women would invite me into the tv room, where, all wrapped up in dressing gowns, they watched rom coms on telly and ate chocolate and giggled, and later on talked of some of the difficulties of life.

Or that nurse who was so good at persuading me to start eating after my three week attempt to never eat again. Somehow she was able to sit with me at the table with my bowl of soup and it was the opposite of a battle, eating wasn't the focus although at the same time it was and I felt no awkwardness if I did or did not eat, but I did enjoy her praise later on, when I did.

I do not know how they do this, these people. I can be so silent, so incapable of connecting and yet different people reached through to me. In the gym, which I went to under protest, there was a lot of silliness, a lot of banter. Later, when I was allowed to the OT room, I just loved making all the various things, I forget what, Christmas cards and wee sculptures. And floating through everything was the bond and the talking that had seemed to have gone away when life became so hard.

It is strange to think back. The admission, three times ago, when I collected twigs and logs from the woods; they, for some reason, were my route to salvation. They symbolised, I no longer know what, but something about safety and nature and a defence against evil, and my friends laughed as I explained this, but they laughed with pleasure and helped me find just the right twigs, and the nurses did not worry about all these things cluttering up my room.

During another admission I decided that if I never slept again and walked and walked, I would breach some barrier and become exalted and pure. So I did walk; round and round the ward for hour after hour. Sometimes one of my fellow patients, who was high, would join me and the nurses did not mind. Even at three in the morning, when I was still walking past all the patient's bedrooms, they did not mind. As long as I did not wake anyone. And when I was almost staggering and my feet were covered with blisters and sweat and my socks full of holes, they were somehow by my side, letting me carry on until I was ready to stop, accepting that at five in the morning I would be up and walking again.

Or that last time when I was nearly off constant Obs and a speech and language therapist came round, talking of this and that, until we ended up setting up a writing group in the hospital. We would go from ward to ward, once I was allowed to other wards, and we would write and talk and drink tea and people would join in and it felt lovely.

Or even that man. I will never forget him. There was a time I was in hospital, and I do not think I was seen as psychotic at that time, but I was speaking about what they would think is silly stuff, about devils and the end of the world and spirits. He sat me down one day, or rather one night, and went through all my dearly held beliefs and dismantled them. I remember I really hated him, that I avoided him ever after, but I remember his pony tail and his earnest desire to make a difference; to take me away from all that tormented me.

That is another thing. Nothing is ever certain or clear cut. I think there is something quite incredibly privileged about hospital. Because if you were totally and utterly determined to die, you probably could do so. I remember all my scheming and thinking about how to escape, I remember keeping my bank card hidden so that I could buy rope, petrol, razorblades. I remember being able to plan how I would die and yet at the same time being terrified of death; knowing without a shadow of doubt that I needed to die and yet thinking how frightening and lonely it would be when I escaped to the hillside and my death. In contrast, hospital contained me, allowed me to act in the most bizzare ways; to try to live out the most dangerous of ideas and yet at the same time keep me safe. There is something strange and liberating and almost warm when life has broken down completely and you no longer really worry about conforming or being responsible.

Life in a psychiatric hospital is not all about control, although it can seem like it. There was the time when the nurses were explaining how they would have to forcibly inject me if I refused to take my depot injection and I did hate that, did cringe at the thought of people manhandling me, poisoning me with their drugs. Yet within all that was visit after visit from the pharmacist, who would pass out leaflets explaining the different drugs and their ways of working and side effects and who would spend ages and ages listening to my anxieties about everything. In the end, I had no choice but to take the depot, but the time before that, I did have control of which of the many different oral antipsychotics on offer I would end up taking.

Just how do I explain hospital? I do not have those good words. Hospital is a place that surrounds me with the worst of life, and sometimes some horrible treatment and some unpleasant people, but within it all are the people who reach through, who hold you in warmth even though you accuse them of being jailors, who give you time even though you are unable to acknowledge them, and who just somehow are there with you despite the huge void you are struggling within.

There was the time that all my friends, with their children and babies, were crowded into my room and my mental health officer came to assess me for something or other, and despite having driven for an hour to get to me, turned round and said it was more important for me to enjoy myself than see her and she left it for another day. Or the chaplain who would listen to me talking about devils while claiming to be an atheist, would listen to my talk of my relationships, give me tissues for my tears, give me books to read.

Yes, I cannot bring the pleasure people gave me in hospital to life because all I can remember is that profound sadness, but I can at least tell you they did give me so much, not the least being my life, even though I struggle to recognise it.

UNDERTHINKING WITH WENDY

We play a game of underthinking. When I am busy, whirling round like a dog chasing its tail. Busy thinking of the *What if?* The *Maybe?* And this and then that and of course, that too, and my head is twisting itself in circles, shocked, like it were placed in ice cold water on a sunny day.

I pause, you pause. We giggle, we underthink. We blame humans for thinking, look to Vonnegut's end of time, when we will bask in a new form with very little brains and a talent for enjoying the sunlight and the meadows and not pondering tomorrow, or even what we think of each other and you and I, we underthink. We slip out of the radiowaves and say,

'What is it that I think?'

Your eyes are bluey-grey, your lips give the best kisses, you are the person I want to be with forever and yet, in a year, a month, a second, it may all be different. But just now, being with you is my heaven. Just now is, is, is.

Just now is my worry that I may fall out of love one day, that I may lose my job, that I may not reach that ideal I cannot express and,

Oh, underthink! Underthink!

I say, 'Get back to the basics.'

I hide under a bush in a dry hollow with crunchy leaves and let the sun dapple me. I distil myself to the very tip of a juniper leaf, the exact end of it. I become the precise centre of a concentric ripple. I become so concentrated that I explode with a sonic boom and shatter the silence of the lochside, our paused breath in bed. I shatter my equanimity, I startle awake clutching you, breathing fast and deeply, laughing a raggedy laugh that says,

'Where did all that calm go?'

I walk in a glade of bluebells, becoming smaller and smaller until I am the essence of the green sea-like light. I am so happy that I have become so little, so unnoticeable until I notice my happiness, my pride, and then I swell into being and see your disappointed smile at the mud on my shoes, the crushed flowers, the fact that I was so busy being infinitesimal that I forgot to lie down here and kiss you and do that underthinking that forgets what underthinking is.

I sit on a rock and stare at the mountains, sit on a log of driftwood and stare at the silver mist of the sea, feel the breeze on my face. Watch a long-legged spider walk over my shoe, see a butterfly fluttering amongst the dusty heather.

I pause, I breathe so deep. I am the sand, I am the air, I am that mite of dust flying in the sun, and then I'm not: I am working out how I will tell everyone, how I will describe my magical connection with oneness. How I will resurrect that old story of being at sea, thousands of miles from anywhere, and I became as tiny as a salt grain, as big as an atom, as small as the universe.

And here I could swear so foully, if I weren't brought up not to swear, and I could accuse myself of forgetting what I am trying to do completely. I could think a glass of whisky this evening will cure this arrogance and think of all the ways I pretend to be clever and feel my stomach curl inside me. Hint that the whisky might come early.

I say to myself and berate myself, 'Deep breaths, soft breaths. Learn to giggle, to play, celebrate those wayward thoughts. Let the frantic thoughts settle like silt in a disturbed puddle that slowly turns clear and peat brown, lit by the amber sun.'

Settle for being me. Settle for being a puppy that is so anxious to please that it gambols up to the biggest, fiercest dog. Settle for being me, who would cook my love a thousand meals, dream up a million poems, laugh a dozen times an hour, resurrect that first kiss at the train station over and over again and delight in the new dream of hope and laughter. Settle for worrying about my complicated filling, my gouty foot, settle for worrying whether I am a good friend, an adequate boss. Settle for lying awake all night as the radio soothes me to sleep and keeps me thinking at the same time. Settle for being me being me; busy blaming, busy worrying, busy craving a thousandfold confirmation of attraction. Settle joyously for me and you and the first stage of the underthinking might just possibly begin.

STARING AT MYSELF FROM THE BOTTOM OF A WELL

Before we separated, became different, became enemies.

How did that happen? I really do not understand. We were joined, for thousands of days we were joined, a partnership. Such a partnership that we knew each other's conversations and knew each other's histories inside out and yet that gap grew, that gap could not be bridged. And with my unpleasantness and my wife's, I do not know what, there was no branch to reach into the river to rescue whoever's hand was reaching out for safety.

My wife always hated the terminology of 'carer'; had insisted, with indignation, that she was my wife, not some therapist, some 'looker-afterer', some jargon-ridden symbol of care. And yet, as my admissions to hospital continued, and as I drifted away; a branch twirling out of reach in an eddie, in a wide dark stream, she started searching out the websites and began sharing things with other carers: husbands, wives, parents, and what she shared made a new kind of sense. It also made her study what she now saw as my illness, my disability, my inadequacy.

It made her see me as something very different to how she used to view me. And maybe my wife was right: that my illness makes it impossible for me to love and share emotion and communicate.

Maybe she was right when she went on those websites and said she now understood me: that love and true humanity are impossible for me. And if she isn't, what could it be that made her want to think that?

Maybe I am. Sometimes when I hear these words I wonder if really I am. Do I really not know emotion? Is it true I don't feel? That I don't know what being human is? Sometimes I worry that I am a psychopath. That I do not connect with others. That maybe she was right, that what she says I am, is something I will never be able to see, because not knowing is part of being me.

When there are books devoted to our difference, our impairment, the myriad ways we fail to function, when people say, 'Your world is not ours, you are not of us,' you can feel unloved, you can feel lonely and uncertain. You can sit and puzzle and think, *What am I really? Am I truly so blind that my reality is no one else's? Am I so blinkered that I do not recognise my otherness?*

Was that man in the airport right? The one who said people like me were scum? That we don't deserve to live? Am I doomed to always be separate and disconnected, not only from me but everyone else? Ah, it is so silly! Such a waste of time. If I am alien and cannot see this then I will not worry about it.

And I will not worry because, even if I am separate, which I must admit I know I am, the last five years have shown me something of a different way of living which allows for my separateness.

I have done my own new growing up with Sarah's Cara and Sally. From the first few weeks of Cara's birth they have been a central part of my life.

It is funny to think about, in a way. I remember that first year. Sarah and me and Jean, doing everything together: chattering, walking, laughing, gossiping and confiding. Those days in Jean's house, full of her artwork and objects from across the world, the sort of quirky, hippy decoration that I strive for, yearn to have and yet have no idea how to create.

All those evenings when, after Ailsa, her daughter, was in bed, she would pop to my part of the house and we would talk and talk and talk and I would drink too much, and because of the drinking I do not know what it is we have actually shared but it has been very special.

And for a time, maybe twice, maybe three times a week, I would cook food at Sarah's house and Jean and Ailsa would come round to share the meals and more talking would take place and more people would come by. And maybe I didn't do so much of the talking but I have been a part of it, I have been a part of people's lives to such an extent and it fills me, fills me with a new confidence.

I love that I have a key to Sarah's door. I love that I babysit Cara twice a week and that over the years I have changed her nappies, brushed her teeth; that I have inspected her bedroom for monsters and that in my house she walked her first steps and in my company did her first wee on a real toilet. I love that Sally used to take photo after photo on my phone and that I took Sally for her first bus journey. I love the ritual we had to go through when getting Cara into her cot and the ritual we needed to go through when getting her changed for bed and how, now, it has changed. That at one point she would not let me leave the bathroom when she was there and nowadays at certain points I have to stand outside but not move completely out of sight.

I love that I have made great big meals at Sarah's house when the children have birthdays, and that it has been important that I make those meals and speak with the people who eat them.

I love the lumpy sofa with the bedspread that falls off it and I love that the dog will climb up on it with me. I love that the cat purrs against me when it is renowned for scratching people. I love and am proud that I sent Sarah out to find a life, apart from babies and work, and I am proud that I was able to see that I would never be her companion and was able to say she needed one. And able to survive when she found someone she could love and who could love her.

I love the evenings when she gets back from her nights out and we sit and talk, maybe with a glass of wine, and I love that we walk with the dog on the beach in all weathers and that in the summer we go round to Jean's house to sit outside at the long table in the garden, overhung with tendrils of some sort of tree, where the dog rushes around; Jean's dad smokes, her mum smiles and it feels like some sort of huge family; full of different, slightly abandoned people.

People like me, still on the edge, still lonely, still convinced they are unlovable, but with others there who are not like that. Lots of shiny, bright, people, lots and lots of single mothers, lots of stray males, lots of children.

It has been a huge waking up so far, a huge brand new adventure and yet, I am still lost, and I still look at my wife's emails at night, even though my new friends will not talk about her at all anymore. I still worry that my wife might be right; that although I can chop asparagus and mix it with tomatoes and mascarpone and gnocchi for my friends, and although I can soothe Cara's tears and used to read Sally bedtime stories, that I am alien, that what I think is love is not love; that what I think is humanity and emotion is some pretence that I am not even aware I am pretending to live.

INDEPENDENCE

We are on our very first foreign holiday together. It is exceptionally exciting, getting the train into Glasgow and then the bus to the airport. Me, worrying all along that we will be too late, checking my tickets and passport over and over again, clutching Wendy's ticket too, happy to feel that somehow I am leading us along on our trip even though she found the hotel, the country, booked the tickets, found out how to get from the airport to the town.

The aeroplane is weird. Wendy holds tightly onto my hand for take off and scrunches her face into my shoulder, making me feel very brave indeed. We share a dark secret: Wendy thinks that if she stops thinking about keeping the plane in the air it will crash, while I think if I think thoughts that are too dark its wings will fall off or its engines fail and we will plummet to the ground. Sharing our worries makes us laugh, almost stops our anxiety.

Gerona is lovely and our cheap weekend at the hotel, amazing. It seems so plush a place. The Catalans are planning an informal independence referendum and have Catalan flags all over the place and various street performances. We want to go up to them and say we will have our own referendum soon too, that maybe in a few months we will be independent.

Across the river, the narrow stone streets, the houses, the sort of dusty smell and coffee. This is beautiful. We have a breakfast of churros at a café, sitting in the street, shaded by trees and in the evening we find a creperie full of noise and laughter and bustle. It even has half of a VW campervan making up some of its décor and place settings with paper and pens to draw on as you wait for your dinner.

Wendy is in a wonderful mood and draws extremely rude pictures on the mats which I, scandalised, scribble over so that the waitress will not see them when she comes by.

This is a new life. I am an accidental prude: when Wendy is being rude and exuberant, when she talks about the wildness her friends have got up to when they have gone out; when she talks frankly and makes jokes about all the numerous things I would never mention without going quiet and pink, I am in heaven. It is like waking up. I don't have to watch my every thought, my footsteps, my movements. I may never learn to be wild but I might lift my voice above a soft murmur. I might swing her hand slightly more exuberantly than normal as we walk up to the castle the next day, I might walk up the castle steps two at a time or even walk on the grass when I am not sure I am allowed to.

SEEKING THE BIG UNTRUTH

I cannot even remember all the different types of medication I have taken over the years. I have almost never taken a medication and had that sense of relief, that feeling of, now I will be ok. Even when I have, I have never wanted it and I do not know why.

I find myself thinking, wondering why so many people hate medication, why people react with that instinctive, 'I don't want medication.'

Why is that? If I had typhoid I wouldn't say, 'I hate these pharmaceutical companies. I hate the thought that this medication makes me better. I will resist that pill till the last moment.'

Over the last wee while, I have been bumping into people who say that their antidepressants, their anti-anxiolitics are lifesavers; how the daily dose of a wee pill keeps them safe, keeps them stable, how they have no need of psychotherapy, no need to immerse themselves in the detritus of the past or the complexity of the future. I see people who say, 'I have an illness. I take a pill, it keeps me well. I am not addicted to it but I do dread the day that the doctor will try to take me off it.'

And I feel some sympathy, some shock, that we have made almost everyone resistant to taking pills that might keep them well.

'Pharma' is an easy target, a lovely place for the angry to take aim, and sometimes with great justification. Pharmaceutical companies do make huge profits, they have done questionable things. They do have great power, they do distort the world of our therapy and the therapy they offer is something that can ruin our lives, but on the other hand, even though the radicals amongst us try to make the case that drugs have no effect at all, other than damage, those drugs seem to give a life to millions of people who would not have that life without that wee cup and the swill of water to shake the pills down.

I still don't really know why I hate medication, why I wish I didn't take it. But sometimes I worry that the only reason I feel this is because I am supposed to feel this, because I have been told to feel this.

So why *do* I hate drugs?

I would like to say I hate drugs because they dull me, they make my life hard to live. I would like to say it is because, when I was taking the injections of Depixol, I always had to walk in circles, to pace the kitchen with that internal restlessness, or because, when I was on Olanzapine, I put on weight and felt that little bit subdued or maybe, when I take Risperdal, I am conscious that it has an effect on my sex drive, that I seemed to develop man boobs, that maybe the fact that I am on the verge of being diabetic is not just a result of lifestyle but a consequence of the medication.

Maybe I would like to say it is because when I take sleeping pills like Zopiclone, I zone out, feel weird, or when I take things like Diazepam or Lorazapam, I feel that temptation to always be in that warm slurry of softness where my feet and legs stop shivering and I cease to worry.

Maybe it was the indignity of hitching my trousers down every two weeks for the jag in my bum from a stranger, or maybe it is because I know exactly what the new jag in my arm will feel like. I know how the different nurses will greet me. I know which nurse will push the needle in so slowly that my muscle clenches and I feel pain or which one will spear me with a quick jab I almost never feel and then say that I don't need a plaster so that now all my favourite shirts have a stain at the shoulder.

I have asked our members in HUG (the group I work with) why they don't like medication and some of their views do chime with mine.

I don't like to feel controlled, I don't like being told what to do. I don't like, above all, to be seen as defective and needing mended. I don't like the implication that if I take medication, I have to admit that there is something wrong with me.

I hate the thought that by taking medication I agree I have an illness. I hate the thought that if I take medication I don't know who I am, that I am masking the real me with the drugs that make me different and acceptable.

137

I hate the fact that by accepting my medication I accept that your view is the right one and mine a petty delusion. I hate the fact that you are right and I am wrong. I hate that now I have seen my notes and the research into my notes that I have to agree I have schizophrenia when I still know this is a mistake; that if ever there is a test for it, when I am tested doctors will say, 'Why no, that is not what he had!'

And I hate the fact that I am anxious about what they might decide I am instead. However, mostly, I hate medication because I am expected to hate medication.

I also hate medication because I know somewhere deep in me, or so I hope to dare to hope, one impossible day I will realise that I am not the devil, that I am not going to bring the world to an end, that if I am incredibly lucky I will be free from this dread and a part of me is terrified of this.

Can I really sit down and say I have lived a life where I know I am the very worst person imaginable? Can I say that and then say, but now that I take medication, however unwillingly, that this thought, fact, belief, reality is uncertain? This bedrock is a quicksand of my own making that has not only dragged me down, but those I love down too? Can I really face up to the fact that I have based my life on a complete untruth – isn't that what taking medication would acknowledge?

And yet I pause. I want to be real, I want to be what I really am, not this fake person and yet I cannot face the real me. I cannot confront this. For me, not taking medication might liberate me and make me real and yet for those around me it would throw me into illness and possible death.

Medication is confusing but I know it keeps many people alive and sane. I think it might do that to me. I also think that it has destroyed countless lives too. I think it is something with a value base we have not really explained to ourselves or each other, except via the soundbites of idealogy.

June

MORECAMBE BAY ADVENTURES

It is really exciting. My love, my treasure, who I want to show to the whole world, to show that I am not quite as boring as even I think I am, my love is off to meet my brother and his family again.

We are driving south to England and the light is the light of summer. We talk. Well, Wendy talks; talks away, chattering, nattering, making the drive bright and fast.

I have finally mastered the sat nav so that it will take me over the Erskine Bridge instead of into Glasgow and I just love the scenery; all these straight fast motorways winding between the hills, between the rain showers.

For a moment I get anxious when I remember that my brother's sitting room stretches up into the rafters and that it might not work with Wendy's fear of high ceilings.

I love the predictability; the hugs when we arrive, Jenny slinking around trying to study for her exams, Louise scowling about something, Harry practicing being adorable.

I even love that we go back and forth to Booths twice with my brother, to collect forgotten ingredients for dinner and the extravagance of that dinner.

The sofa bed we sleep on, on the sort of mezzanine floor above the dining room, is wonderfully soft. Through the windows we can see a hot air balloon, almost motionless in the sky. I can almost imagine that I hear the roar of the burner that keeps it aloft.

And it is predictable that in the morning my brother and Sharon argue where we should go for our walk, round and round they go, discussing the pros and cons of how frequently visited and how far away, the familiarity makes me glow.

We go to the sea, to the mudflats of Morecambe Bay. My brother drives very fast indeed and I have no idea where I am meant to be going, so the journey consists mainly of me asking Wendy where he has got to; trying to catch him up, keep him in sight.

It is unfair of me to have agreed to this day trip. Wendy is not a clambering over rocks, getting covered in mud sort of person, and here mud stretches as far as you can see, gleaming with bright patches of sea along runnels and lakes made by the tide. The dog turns grey and is joined by the children who also turn grey, but most of us clamber over the boulders. Wendy grabbing moments to say she is never going to go bouldering again in her life, me reaching out to provide an arm for wee jumps down, teasing her.

We eat lunch on the grass above the sea, where the small yellow and red flowers are, where the daisies grow and the sheep droppings dry amongst the compact thistles and the bristly grass.

The sky is blue summer. Wendy likes my brother, likes his wife, his children, and I can now visit him with some joy in my mind. I can do that laughing that she brings to me so often and so naturally. And that apartness that has made the last few visits slightly edged, slightly caught on the sight of these lovely people doing the stuff I would like to do, slightly caught on my loneliness, my apartness, the absence of my own family, has gone. I am not apart. I am not here to be talked about. I do not need my brother to look after me, to protect me. I need nothing more than my ability to love and be loved.

MEMENTOS

Under the stairs was a large canvas case. It was my memory box before memory boxes were invented. It was full of things: my wife's letters to me, my diaries, scraps of writing, postcards, letters from my mum and others. Old memorabilia, magazines I had appeared in, brochures we had created. That sort of thing.

A treasure trove of my early adulthood.

I stopped adding to it some time ago. It just sat there waiting for those times when I would pull it out and gaze at the past: recollect, feel, muse, reflect.

In the office was my certificate for my MBE and the medal itself, and my birth certificate and my exam certificates and qualifications. There was my pension and my job applications and my invites to important things, the history of our last twenty five years.

In the shed were my skis and my bike.

In the porch were my walking boots and my wellyboots and my scarves and my coats.

On the walls and throughout the house were the paintings we had gathered. Upstairs was the sequence of framed photos from India and the wedding photos.

In our son's room was my forty-seven-year-old teddy.

In the kitchen was the pressure cooker we bought when we moved to Edinburgh.

In the hall was the carved wooden bookcase from recycled wood we had commissioned a few years ago.

In the sitting room was the address book with all our friends from around the world in it.

There was the sofa we bought that was exactly the same as my brother's, which we laughed about twenty years ago.

There was the rug we bought in Edinburgh, the palm frond we called 'stick' that we took back from Morocco.

There were the posh glasses we bought and were given and the old coffee tin you bought back from Amsterdam for my coffee.

There was the stereo our son pooed on when I was in hospital.

In the shed were all the tools I used to build shelves and make shelters; there was the lawnmower you hated that we used for the lawn and the axe we had just bought from Norway to split wood.

The candles, lots of candles, the aromatherapy oil heater.

The coffee grinder John gave us which I used for spices.

The knives and bowls and crockery we had built up over the decades.

The music we collected over twenty five years.

A whole history. A history of me, you, our son, our friends and families. A whole precious history.

I don't understand why you would destroy everything that belonged to me and keep everything precious and commonplace that belonged to you and both of us, and not let me have any of it at all.

I don't understand why I was wiped out of everything as though I never existed. I don't understand why I was removed from the lives of my sisters-in-law, my nieces and nephews and my mother-in-law.

I don't understand why none of my side of the family was ever again told a single thing about our son's life.

I don't understand why you kept on telling them to stop writing to him.

I don't understand.

How could you do it?

THE SCENT OF SWEET PEAS

I looked at the house next to Ash's to see if I could buy it, some time ago. It was just about right but slightly too expensive. I had all sorts of plans for it and took my friends round: Sarah, Jean, Murray. It had been on the market for ages and ages and I dared to put in a reasonable offer, or so I was told, but it wasn't accepted. I stare into its empty rooms each time I pass it in the narrow vennel in which it is sited.

Ash's house is lovely. I met her when one of my friends was doing a reading at the bookshop in Nairn and we have been talking ever since.

Just as with my next door neighbour, she often comes round about tea time. If it is good weather we will sit outside sipping wine and eating nibbles, drinking whisky later.

We talk of this and that, often about her many, many years of living in the Netherlands, often of her son in Hong Kong and often of her writing which she is so good at. And often of I am not sure what, long conversations about gender and living and generally being.

Today you have come to visit and we are sitting in her garden across the street from her house, drinking coffee. The cat is there, there is a profusion of flowers, the washing on her line is making lovely shapes in the wind which I am trying to photograph with my camera.

I am doing my usual. Soon we will set off for Muir of Ord and later on, to Dingwall. Taking you round all the people I know, showing you them, showing them you. This evening you will turn to me and ask me not to introduce you to so many people in one day and I will promise not to, knowing that next time you are with me I will have thought of more people I want you to see, all full of the excitement of you; the confusion that this has happened, that life is changing so much that I nearly always look forward to the morning, that I can actually think of people to take you to see.

FORGIVE ME ALL OF YOU – PLEASE

I have forgotten the effect I had on my family and maybe never did know it.

My wife came into hospital every day, when the world went wrong after my son was born; wheeling our son up in his buggy, being there for me, drained and shocked and traumatised. And still being cheerful and loving and on my side. Planted firmly in my life, in my world; reaching through to me. Holding me, even though I didn't know it. Holding me in her mind even though, for weeks, I refused to touch her or my son because I thought I would infect her with my evil.

I am still not sure what those two years did to my wife and my son. I do not know.

I have never sat by someone I love with all my heart and wondered whether the next day that person will have killed themselves. I have never been laughing with someone I love, taking a rare break by the shore in Leith, having a drink on the quayside while our son sleeps peacefully in the car, only to have to hear that love suddenly reveal that the beautiful sparkles on the water are spirits staring at him, warping his thoughts, that he needs to go back to the house, that he needs to be with the sacredness of the wood and the soil.

That he will live under the floorboards of the house and fight a battle with the evil spirits, that there is nothing wrong with him but this fight and that he needs no help and no medication and that it will be all alright.

As I write this I am aghast at how blind I am at what I did.

I have spent a page or so saying that my wife was abusive in some ways and so, if she was that, what was I?

What was I when I would sit blankly, sullenly in the chair at home, on those rare occasions when I agreed to come up out of the dirt and the dark, dressed up in oilies and hats because they were protecting me from the thoughts that were being altered by the spirits? And she would sit and try to persuade me to eat.

What was I doing when I would try to stub cigarettes out on my hands only to be stopped by the sobs of my wife begging me not to?

What was I when I refused medication, refused to go to hospital and then decided to go to hospital after all, only to be held back by my wife who said she would love me, look after me, keep me safe, keep me from the horrors I went into when I was in hospital?

And she did keep me safe, did stop me from descending, full flood into terror. And she looked after our son when he would toddle up to the trapdoor I used and point down and say,

'Daddy.'

She would hold our son when I would look at him and burst out crying, and she would hold me later when I would allow myself to be held, and is it any wonder that she was exhausted and tired and angry?

Is it any wonder that as those years went by she found herself with someone she loved but thought of as alien, as a stranger? Someone, who, now he was on medication, and who, when she cuddled up to him at night, she found even smelled different?

Is it any wonder that she became more distant when I was held back in the hospital after attending the day clinic, having been found with a razor blade, about to cut my wrist; speaking to them, convincing them that she had the strength, the ability to look after me at home. That being away from family, being confined to a ward would only make me worse, make my existence all that more terribly risky, that much more a matter of life and death.

That she would be strong again and in between caring for and loving my son, bringing laughter into his life, she would be there for me. The person she no longer knew but who she loved and treasured and who she so much wanted to come back to her, to come back to her as the gentle, skinny, smiley, passionate person she once knew.

It is a strange thing to be writing this. To be thinking that someone devoted themselves to loving me, to looking after me and that far from loving her back, I grew distant and resentful, drew away, became grudging, became angry at the way she treated me, used another person to complain about her, became close to that person and then just gave up on her, blamed her for everything and walked away.

I can see now the bitterness that would come from that leavetaking.

I think of my son. I think how he must have felt so confused the next time I went into hospital. I do not know how old he would have been. Maybe fourteen.

I think of all those confused feelings. I think that I had asked to be put on a new drug called Abilify. And, at first, it made me feel so, so, wonderful. I became more alert, more vibrant, more engaged and more lively and cheerful. It seemed like something amazing. Sitting in the office talking to my psychiatrist; babbling, laughing, saying, 'Life is great, is wonderful now.'

And my wife, smiling too, holding my hand, leaning in to me and saying now, after all these years, she had at last got back the person she married.

Both of us smiling, feeling lovely and loving. And yet with the joy came the other side of it.

The energy spilled into being awake, being wide awake at two in the morning and three in the morning and four in the morning. In the evenings, going for long, long, walks in the frost-glittery streets. Starting to write and finding that if the nights are going to be wakeful I may as well write through them.

And the realisation that this is not right, that I cannot exist on no sleep at all or at best, a couple of hours. Phoning for advice on what to do and finding no one who could help and such a lack of knowledge of this new drug, that we were made helpless.

As the nights fled by, the energy I had became more and more brittle, my eyes just that bit red-rimmed, my feelings more on the edge of a-tremble, and those thoughts of the devils and the evil and the ooze of badness inside me more and more a part of me.

I remember I didn't tell my wife. Once I would have been open and easy and trusting with this truth but now I kept it to myself. Began again to think of death and self-destruction, began to feel that I was at the critical point where the devil in me would take me over, consume me completely.

And then I was in hospital.

It is strange that I cannot remember a time so intense and extreme. These times blur into my memory. It all becomes much the same. I would have been doing the usual, wanting to harm myself, wanting to kill myself.

My son visited. Said the room I had was fab. Said he wanted to stay in the one next to me. Laughed a lot, made jokes. Hugged me.

I can't remember how we explained it to him, if I even did. I remember we talked of me being there because I couldn't sleep, but he is not stupid. He is more perceptive and aware than I have ever been.

And then again.

I cannot believe it. Cannot believe I was so stupid. Some months later I asked to go back on the Abilify again. I wanted to do it with more supervision and a gradual shift from the Olanzapine to the Abilify.

I wanted not to be the stranger any more. I wanted to be loving and I wanted to be loved and I wanted a life again. I wanted a life again. That drug promised me a life.

And the same thing happened. I was given diazepam to help me sleep, I was assigned a CPN or maybe I already had her, I don't know.

Over the months I became more and more tired and more and more messed up, more and more all the things I don't want to be. Just exhausted, with a mind that is trembling with tiredness, can't go another step, no longer knows how to think, to consider, to reflect or to relax.

My notes say I stopped taking it eventually but that is not my memory.

There came a time when my CPN was arranging for me to go back into hospital and I was agreeing, accepting this needed to happen.

It is strange to be giving a speech at a national conference and knowing that the next day you will be in hospital, and to look at those people who just don't get it.

I had always been admitted to hospital as an emergency before. I remember vividly standing with my bags packed, in the porch, hugging my wife goodbye and bursting into tears, holding her and not wanting to leave. I remember driving up the road to the hospital, through the hills. Taking my hand from the steering wheel to wipe my eyes free of the tears that were making my vision blurry and walking down the corridor with my bags, thinking, *What am I doing?*

And was it that time? When we were sitting at opposite ends of a bench seat, waiting for a ward round, leaning as far away from each other as possible, my hair and my clothes rank. My wife steaming anger at everything, dreading the resumption of the years of sadness, hating all the professionals, hating it all. Tight-lipped and exhausted and drained, unable to speak to me.

As the papers for my detention came through, she asked not to be sent them, wanted no phone call, no letter, nothing to do with all this, and still they sent them.

Finally, after weeks, my psychiatrist reached through to her, listened to her and gradually she agreed to speak with him, to sometimes phone the ward, to be a part of my treatment. For me, his acceptance of her point of view alienated me from him.

When he nodded his head and said I was a complex case, a complicated individual, I grew weary and as some of his personal ethics and personal judgements began to spill into his care, I lost my liking for him.

I don't know anything anymore.

I wonder how they all felt? It must be exhausting watching someone who has lost himself, who doesn't know what he does to those around him.

When I am in that place where I am wanting to die, I rarely think beyond that. The world I am in is a place of intensity and self-obsession and different forms of logic; things make sense to me in ways that they do not to other people and death becomes both terrifying and liberating. And sometimes, in some of the places I get to, I do not realise that my physical death would be a real death. I am almost caught inside a story from which I cannot escape.

I remember the student nurse who spoke with me the first night of one of my hospital admissions. I was busy writing, not making much sense as I had been awake for maybe two days in a row. I find it hard to believe people when they say that they haven't slept for a week because when I really haven't slept for a few days there is little that is left of me.

Anyway, I was saying how much I wanted to die and how necessary for the world it was that I died and she talked to me, in that dark night, in the bright lights of the dining area about, how, as a child, her mum had wanted to die and of how hurt she was and wounded and damaged. And she talked of my son, of how my death would be something he would never recover from, that it would become central in his life, something he measured everything against. That it would be the worst, most terrible thing I could do to him. For a moment I understood but it was many weeks before I stopped trying to kill myself.

I think of the time I left the hospital, at night, in the middle of a great storm in which people on the west coast died. I left the hospital to buy razor blades from the Co-op down the road in the town and in seconds I was soaked to the skin as the rain lashed and the wind roared.

As I walked to the Co-op my phone rang. It was my mum asking how I was, asking what all the noise was and as I walked I said there was no problem, no reason for the noise.

The Co-op was closed. So I turned round and walked back to the hospital and arrived just as the police were about to be called. I think it was the next morning that I was sectioned.

Even though I am saying these words, I don't know.

I remember the time I was in hospital and even though I was on constant observations I had been able to pick up a drinks can from the ward that I had smuggled into my bed. In the dim of the lights I had been able to, with great care and patience, work it back and forth until it split in two and the halves were sharp and bright against my skin while the nurse sat at my door reading whatever the latest magazine would have been.

In the middle of the night, maybe two in the morning, my phone rang.

153

It was my sister, who never speaks to me when I am in hospital because she cannot bear it and does not understand or know what to say. But this night she had had an overwhelming feeling that I was in huge danger and had reached across the country and the night to speak to me in my hospital room with my sharp-edged Coke can.

So, when she spoke to me, I told her what I was doing and agreed to pass the can to the nurse on the door. And I don't know what she would have felt when she hung up the phone. I know I felt her love reaching out to me.

I remember my brother shouting down the phone at me when I laughed one evening at how good it would be when I am finally free of my community treatment order. How I laughed and said I would then be able to stop my medication, and he shouted and said, did I not know what it was like? What it was like to spend day after day waiting for that final phone call that said I was dead, did I not know what I was doing to my family?

In so many ways I do not know. It is only at rare times like this, that those words reach through to me, bring me up short with a guilty lump in my throat.

I think of the time when my brother, after a long week at work, drove up to visit me. A drive of over 300 miles, driving through a terrible blizzard to see me in the hospital. Arriving in time to give me a quick hug before going to my flat, to take one look at my bed and decide it would be better to sleep on the floor. And how in the morning I looked at him, thin and fit and exhausted and how I told him how I was in a battle of good and evil and because I was the evil person in that battle, the good thing would be my death or some such thing, and I think I remember a hug before he left to drive all that way home again. I remember thinking how hard and taut his body was, thinking I have grown flabby.

When I was released he took me shopping, bought me knives and bowls and pans and chopping boards and I was overjoyed at this generosity, so happy that it would now be easy to cook. I remember how we walked for what seemed like hours along the beach, arguing about medication and looking after myself and not drinking so much and getting fit and eating well and washing.

Ah, I think I am glad my memory is a bit hazy about these times. I think somehow I need to give thanks to those who have loved me.

I have never really known how much I have been loved and how much I have hurt. It sometimes feels as if I have ambled through my life, feeling the brief touch of those who care for me and love me and I look back with a blank heart saying,

'Why do you love me?'

Or maybe worse than that, staring back with a blank heart and not even noticing that love, being oblivious, not believing for a moment that I am lovable, not dreaming that people could care about me, worry about me. Not knowing that there are people who are wounded by me. Not knowing that people have shared a journey with me, and I have not noticed that they were holding me and treasuring me while I was losing even me from me.

I ask myself why my wife would ever have hit me, would ever have hated me, would ever have despaired of me, would ever have hurled words at me, and I think I now understand. I think I let her love me for years and years in the way of sorrow and I let that love slip away from me. Just walked out with a glow in my heart that I was free.

July

A HOLIDAY OF FUTURES

A sparrow landing on my foot, mid conversation. Pausing, both it and me astonished. I claim I am a natural animal attractor person.

Hitching the blue poppies to the wall, accompanying them with yellow ones. Forgetting to water them.

Taking out dish after dish for four people: tomatoes, chickpeas, aubergines, green beans, courgettes, broad beans and carrots; gram flour and bulgur wheat, cayenne and garlic, cumin and cinnamon. A large jug of fruit juice and vodka, the orange and lime skins in the bin.

Lying in the dark with the window open, feeling warm air on my chest, listening to seagulls.

Watching fish jump in the river, sitting at the tables by the harbour, eating scrambled egg and drinking coffee.

Peering at flowers: yellow ones, blue ones, purple ones, pink, indigo, violet. Ferns flashing scraps of sun from their surface, glitters of water through the trees. Sitting on the rocks, reading a book while small trout slip by in the tawny water.

Seeing my brown hand on the whiteness of your thighs. You saying, 'That looks kinky!'

Lying on the bed, you at one end, me at the other, the breeze through the velux windows cooling us. The crows bustling outrageously in the fir trees across the road. Talking and talking, while the evening rushes by; we thought time was suspended.

Stretching out in bed, feeling all its corners with my limbs, thinking, *How will we both fit in here later in the year?*

Batting away the midges that aren't really there, scratching at the cleg bite, feeling liquid running down my leg. Keeping to the shady side of the town's streets, visiting a dark bookshop, sitting outside, drinking coke in the sunshine. Contemplating Mull of Kintyre cheddar and laughing.

Making plans, holding hands, getting sweaty.

Making tea, all the guests waiting. Wiping my wet face, my damp hair, insisting on a shower and coming to the room feeling light.

Waking to the haar, the coldness of a summer's day when the rest of the country is bright.

Splashing in the water, letting the waves ride up our legs, feeling the stark coldness, the sun-speared lightness, the rub of shells and gravel on our toes.

Pausing for kisses.

Pausing for more kisses.

Listening to the tractors from our glowing tent.

Cooking 'eggy bread' every day, going for walks every day. Having threads of jokes that reconnect each pausing moment.

Talking, and not noticing cars on single track roads. Watching the sea and the beaches, the cotton-grass and the sand fleas. Making more plans.

Circling round our knowing, circling round our belonging, circling round our confusion, laughing at my age, planning fitness games, planning where my clothes will go, planning a future when we have only just reached the present.

Planning how to break free from our dreams into new ones, planning and giving the gift of trust, the gift of knowing it might wither one day, and still being able to sit on the planks on the terrace and discuss the garden we will sit in, in the evenings.

Paddling in the surf and listening to our pasts taking new form and meaning, seeing multiple acts of tenderness and hoping I deserve them.

Thinking, *Is this real?*

Work starts next week. The future is like the blur of heat in the hot air, the future is a heat haze, filled with the desire for new beginnings, and endings left behind to fade.

Thinking, *Is this real?*

And knowing that next week I will be greeting you with a kiss. Already beginning to gabble with new stories. New things to share with you.

IT IS THE STANDING THAT CHANGES IT ALL

The ward rounds happened once a week when I was in hospital. I must admit that I can't remember them clearly, but I do remember the hanging around, that waiting that could last most of the day until the doctors decided it was time to see you. They would have the pre-meeting about me and then I would be summoned in and would sit in a chair which, although it was part of the circle, was somehow in front of them.

After I had done my bit and answered their questions, I would be sent out and they would discuss me all over again. I did tend to feel like I was a not particularly pleasant exhibit that they had come to discuss and on top of that, although I was meant to participate and join in, it did feel like they had a clear idea of how they would like me to participate. Somehow, the subtext seemed to be about pleasing them, about wanting the same thing as them and that dissent would just make their job more difficult and time-consuming.

It felt like I was being prodded at, inspected, scrutinised, and that often I did not really live up to expectations, in fact, I think they often felt a deep disappointment in me, a weariness at my contrariness.

One ward round, I spent the days before it writing down a series of wishes and wants and statements before attending. I had decided that I knew what should be done and I had decided that they needed to listen to me and act on what I had said. I spent ages in a wee franticness of writing what I wanted to say. I can't remember much of what I did say. I know I asked for the right to self harm, I know I asked for them to let my friend, who worked in the hospital, to be allowed to continue giving me Reiki, and I almost certainly would have been suggesting to them that they went ahead and drained my blood away. I probably asked to be allowed out to walk in the hospital grounds too.

The day of the ward round, I was full of anticipation but when I aired my points and demands and questions I found myself hesitant and nervous and halting, acting like a wee rebellious schoolboy in front of the headmaster.

I do remember that they didn't agree to anything I asked. Some of my points they ignored, some they just said no to, and a few things they explained why they were saying no.

It is that sense of pleading I remember. It feels wrong, now that I think of it. To be a grown man pleading in front of five or six strangers, who all have a power to grant or dismiss what you ask for.

I accepted it at the time, but now that I think of it, surely there must be some other way? I know that I needed protected, looked after. I know that I, in some ways, agreed to give my personal responsibility away, but I am over fifty. Why am I sometimes having to ask a nurse of twenty-two for permission to make some toast? Why am I being told that there will be no more butter in the fridge that day because the patients have eaten too much? Why do I have to have decaf coffee? Why is the milk stopped because they want to stop someone else from drinking too much? And why is my tea time at five in the evening when normally I don't eat until seven or eight? And why do I have no say or power over any of this?

I suppose, like any system, there are ways of doing things and that sometimes the needs of the organisation surpass those of the individual, but in these places we are alert to the signs of being dehumanised and processed. Sometimes I would prefer a degree of chaos to enliven the routine of running a ward smoothly and efficiently. And yet, of course when we are delicate and when we are fragile that very chaos, which may enliven and invigorate, can also cause uncertainty and anxiety.

But it does feel like you become so servile, so dog-like. Never quite sure what you were and were not allowed to do. Never at ease with your own behaviour and so often seeking approval from the staff that surround you. So aware that there were indeed rules and that although being transferred to the IPCU, with its locked doors, or being sent away home to a cold home, or being given the freedom to do such and such was supposed to be done on the basis of our illness and our need. But there is, in the back of your mind, a feeling, because you don't actually feel ill, that you are always being monitored and that if you behave in certain ways, certain things are likely to happen. Nothing so crude as reward and punishment but sometimes, sometimes it almost feels like that.

And those ways of being. I used to write on my laptop and very much wanted the staff to read what I wrote, but the only time they did pay an interest in that writing was when they decided that I was writing about the other patients and said that they would take my computer off me if I mentioned anyone in any way that could identify them.

I remember being indignant at that, that they thought I would expose my fellow patients, but also that they thought patients were bound by the same codes of confidentiality that staff are. There is no law that says we have to keep the workings of the NHS secret, that we cannot make stories out of our time in hospital, or at least I don't think there is. And anyway, the things, we, as patients, shared: we were there for months, some of us. Of course we shared our stories, our secrets, our dreams and phone numbers and indeed, our thoughts about all the different members of staff around us. It is strange that people could try to prevent us from engaging in this everyday gossip and sharing of thoughts and feelings and ideas about the world we found ourselves in.

I suppose that this is turning into a moan about a place that saved my life and that is so hard to explain. It is difficult to be positive about a place where my freedom was limited and my actions limited, and where some of the staff really didn't seem to want to be there and yet, and yet that place and those staff and that stay there means that I am now able to type away today: to walk out the door and see the seagulls and the clouds and feel the harsh wind. I have to remember that too. I do need to.

But now I am back in those memories I remember that, despite the unrelieved boredom that characterises a place like that, that we participated in the tragedies and the dramas too.

I remember this young woman who used to go to the gym with some of us. She hardly ever spoke, but we had a connection, she would arrive just after us in the morning, on the crutches she had used since she jumped from the top floor of a car park some months before.

Over the weeks we all got to know her, we would share glances and grins and the occasional short sentence. She had a whole host of restrictions on her but somehow managed to work a gap out in her surveillance and catch a taxi back to the car park in town, where this time she carried out her wish and jumped again and this time she died.

I remember how the rumours started straight away among the patients. Somehow, we had become close to her. I remember one person crying in the telly room and another crying somewhere else and all the time we were asking the nurses what had happened.

At first they wouldn't even admit that she had died and they never did tell us how it was she died, they said it was confidential and that they couldn't tell us.

I remember the incomprehension, the confusion that someone we had spent an hour a day with for the last couple of months, and who we all knew, was dead. We were not allowed to know anything about it and because we were not allowed to know about it we could not talk about it with the nurses and were discouraged from talking about it with each other.

Then there was the young guy who was filled with anxiety. He would join in with us one moment and not the next, he would say he wanted to die and then that he wanted to get better, he would say that he was gay and then that he wasn't gay, he would talk about what the church thought of gay people and get into a terrible state, caught between the teachings of his own fundamental Christianity and his own nature.

I remember he was very welcome when he came to watch films with us in the telly room or joined us for tea, but that often he would take a wee panic and disappear away back to his room.

He loved the crafting and the pottery, but often threw what he created away.

This young man made a lovely bowl with a metallic glaze and great wavy sides. This one he liked and even agreed not to destroy.

He killed himself not long after being discharged. Sometimes his bowl is still used by the creative writing group and I can feel a faint shudder when I come across it unexpectedly, knowing no one else knows its history.

I have read in books that war is mainly tedium interspersed with intense action and in some ways the ward was like that. Nothing much happened and no one had the energy to make much happen. It was mainly watching telly and waiting for mealtimes or just lying on your bed and sleeping and yet at different points there could be sudden crisis: the alarms might go and the nurses rush to a room where someone had just hurt themselves, a person might be arguing about not being allowed out the doors at the ward entrance, or sometimes it was more the tension in people, the jigger up and down of someone's legs, the touch of tiredness in someone's face, or maybe it was the silence. I suppose that was it. I remember the silence more because I remember so clearly those times when a group of patients might be laughing together and talking away, it is the rarity of that that I remember most of all, now that I think of it. And at the same time that bond you sometimes built up with fellow patients, where you feel so close and where, in witnessing each other, you have inevitably been so intimate with each other and when it is time to leave you are so convinced that you will keep in contact and yet usually, by and by, the connection drifts away.

It is a unique world that some of us revisit again and again and which we cannot really convey to others who haven't experienced it.

August

AT THE SHOWIES

I cannot hear you! The music is beating its way to the clouds above. It is all around me. It is inside me. Inside my ears, filling them so I see your lips moving but I cannot understand what you are saying. We walk, hand in sweaty hand. Way, way above me, at the top of a pole running with throbbing lights, sit people waving their legs into space, waiting to turn and tumble round and round in the black night sky, wee stick insects, arms and legs flailing.

Everywhere there are the cries and screams of excited teenagers, whirling and twirling on garish poster girl, light-popping, music-shouting machines. We walk on the grass, hand in sweaty hand, watching, dodging the drunk people, the crowding people, looking at the hot dogs and the onions and the chips.

Saying to each other, 'We don't want to go on the dodgems!'

And both feeling a twinge of regret that we are so scaredy.

On the road home the ground is littered with plastic pint glasses from the Nairn Highland games, a man sways up the road talking loudly to himself. We kick the glasses down our street, giggle at our loutishness and slip inside my doorway to kiss and cuddle. Outside, the music pounds, lights flash in the sky, poles turn end over end with people at the extremities, octopus hands twist round and round and up and down with screaming people clutched in their bucket seats while, in the safety of my home, we talk and cuddle the night away.

In the morning it's all packed up; the large articulated lorries are already away down the road, leaving patches of yellow grass; a few remnant caravans, vans and lorries remain. The huge dodgem ride has been packed into the length of a long trailer, the generators are being disconnected. People are walking their dogs. Beach visitors are parking their cars where the Aberdeen Angus stand was, buggies are being pushed where the zorbs and the houses of fun were, a scant few hours ago.

On the East beach, we walk with the wind flailing your hair all over your face. The sand rushes in plumes towards Forres. We walk, hand in sweaty hand. Your shoes fill with beach and we sit in the lee of a sand dune. You lay your head on my lap while I take pictures of the harbour light through the marram grass, listen to the sound of the waves, the rustle of the reeds, the cry of the seagulls. Sun strips rush across the beach, light up ships in the firth, pied wagtails flit between the dunes. I stroke your shoulders, look at your hair flickering in the breeze. Remember our kisses, our laughter, our desire, our conversation as the dawn broke.

Walking back, into the wind, the sand flicks into our eyes, you try to walk backwards and fail. At home we lie in bed and I listen to the sound of your breathing, the occasional twitch of your leg or your arm. The weight of your head on my chest. The feel of your hair on my cheek. I lie still, listening to the seagulls, trying not to wake you when I move to look at the bedside clock. I lie still and I think of the showies and of how we should have gone on the dodgems. I lie still and think I am becoming a teenager all over again, but this time with the fun mixed in.

THE BLUE BENCH

When I think back to those first few months after leaving hospital; well, maybe not those first few months, maybe those first few years, maybe even now.

I like to think of the times I spent sitting with my friend, Jean, on the blue bench outside my part of the house. It was a slightly falling apart blue bench, but here we would sit when it was sunny and drink tea and talk of this and that, just this and that; a waft and flow of conversation that I cannot quite remember but which seemed as warm and soft as the sun does on a summer's day when you are in your shirt sleeves and feel only softness and gentleness on your skin.

While we talked on the bench we would remark on the wasps gouging lines out of the wood of the fence between her part of the house and mine.

Her dog, which we called 'the Moog', would rush all over the garden, pausing to dig holes in the grass or to leap onto one of our laps or sit under the bench between our feet, panting a little, maybe with a wee soft toy between her paws.

Sometimes she would poke her head down the strange hole at the edge of the garden, a manmade shaft that we could not find the end of; could not feel with a broom handle or hear a stone reach the bottom of. We made up weird stories of what it might lead to.

The Moog was wonderful. She was often mistaken for a he, being a dishevelled heap of black fur that rushed everywhere.

In the mornings she would nose open my door and leap onto me in my bed. In the evenings when I was sitting doing nothing she would climb onto my lap and rest along my legs, making me feel loved.

She became such a source of conversation. She was always stealing things from me. I kept my food on some blue shelving in the wee conservatory that led into my house and she would come in and lick the

175

labels off the tins, leaving me with no idea what I might be eating that night.

One morning Jean woke up and saw her rushing round the garden dragging my huge bag of mung beans behind her, spilling a river of beans everywhere. Another time we found she had eaten a bag of raw polenta and assumed she might expand till she burst.

She had a liking for my clothes too. She would come by and creep into my bedroom and make off with socks and things. I remember once, when we were talking on the blue bench, we watched the Moog dig up a blackened bundle of material from the garden. It turned out to be a pair of my pants, just one of many socks and things that disappeared, usually never to be found again.

I had forgotten that I have had some good times, some really good times since moving here. I have been introduced and included into a community. Although I walk along quite separately and stand almost always on the edge of conversations, I think I am seen by some people with some affection. I notice that some people I hardly know smile at me when I pass and although I sometimes keep my face blank because I am surprised that they know me and am anxious that they might want me to talk, I am also pleased that in these streets there are people who know where I live and what I do and who my friends are.

And yet still there is an emptiness in me. I try to see me within me and I cannot find me. I don't recognise me in the warmth that people offer me. I wonder how long I have been alone. Sometimes when I think back I cannot remember a time when I felt a part of things.

As I think of this I find myself tumbling back to boarding school, remembering that first year when I was nine and I knew no one and understood little. I had no one at all to turn to or talk to and I remember how I had to become strong, or what people call strong. How I had to force myself not to miss my mum and dad. You had to be strong enough that people would not pick on you because the horrible, horrible thing is that the children did pick on those who were weak and vulnerable.

You had to be alone and self-sufficient and you had to know that affection was a rare thing and support unexpected. You had to steel yourself against trust and the comfort of companionship and so you became alone and, I suppose, a bit lost.

In fact, for the first time in many days my throat has closed on itself at those memories. Maybe most people deal with being sent away easily but I did not cope with it very well at all, although I expect many people would think that I did. Often I was seen as warm and affectionate although some of my school reports have said that I was so lethargic that they wondered if I had lapsed into a coma. My memory is of being alone, of wishing someone could give me a cuddle. I remember my bewilderment at having to go back each break time to learn how to make a bed properly, my confusion that we seemed to be learning a brand new way of writing, just that dislocation from home to an institution where the rules were new and the words alien and the people strangers I did not ever really get to know.

And here in Nairn, now that I am approaching late middle age, I find that I am included in gossip and probably gossiped about. I know that if I knew how to socialise, at even some sort of minimal level, I would be welcomed by people around me. I reach out a bit with this thought. I think how all the woman friends greet each other with a hug and how they tend to include me in this. I like that very much.

These last few months are, and this story is, about this, I think. In my solitude, having to learn how to live again, I am not able to drift in a comfortable fog of nothing much any more. I have to recognise that I crave friendship and that I crave conversation and I need to recognise that I do not need others to look after me. That when the telly aerial falls off I have to organise its repair; that when the paint on the windows blisters, I need to repaint them and find the motivation to do so and that when my stomach is hollow with anxiety, because I am so lonely and so lost and so frightened of what I have done, that I need to do that reaching out to people, risk that rejection and that tongue-tied silence and, not only make friends, but believe that people can and want to be friends with me.

Ah, I struggle with that! Why would anyone ever want to be friends with someone like me? Why would anyone ever seek me out? It is beyond my comprehension and yet, if I want anything approaching the life I dream of, I need to learn that connection and maybe one day learn that self belief.

September

CROSSING CONTINENTS

I am drifting in a haze of Powerpoint, my legs restless, my bum sore, my mind colliding with the sawdust phrases.

I see dandelion parachutes drifting in the summer's breeze, floating beyond my head and over the sand of the beach, caught by a zephyr and whirled high in the sky across the ocean.

To cross the ocean where graphs don't live, to float silent in the night, invisible in a maze of stars, the moonlight catching on them, the sea gleaming below, in a line of white and black shimmering streaks, the flying fish whizzing in the dark, just the sound of them and the sudden clunk as they hit the deck of a ship.

To drift past islands where there are no bullet points and sudden smiley faces, past islands where small waterfalls drape themselves around moss-covered cliffs and waves make the rocky shores silently white.

To reach the edge of a desert where mice don't click and there are no quivering arrowheads, where the sandstorms almost overwhelm them and the sun almost dries them out, where the horizon shimmers with a crust of water, where even the ants seek the shade.

And finally, to cross the savannah where no microphones hum and no figures oscillate; to cross the savannah and dip into a thunderstorm of pure black cloud and crystal water. To be caught by a rain drop, to fold up inside it and plummet through the sky to land with a cold gasp on your shoulder.

You dab at it, dab at it and look and say, 'Where on earth could that have come from?' And I whisper, 'From me. When I blew the dandelion clock and made a wish and closed my eyes to the endless talk and the screen in front of me.'

SEEKING THE SMOOTHNESS, THE SILENCE

I looked through my notes with my CPN the other day, at the records of all those years that I have seen psychiatrists. For many years it seemed there was little need for me to see those psychiatrists. I was fine, maybe a bit worried, maybe a bit anxious, a scrap depressed, maybe working too hard. But all the way through it was this thread of alcohol.

I had never known how much a part of the way that they look at me and write in their notes about me involves alcohol.

It was something exciting and forbidden when I was young. It was that wee, excited sip from a glass from your parents in the summer and trying to pretend you liked it.

It was learning that you get a taste for it. That the more you try it the less horrible it will be and the better it will taste. What is it? You develop a palate or something? It seems to me today, with my faintly muzzy head, that fresh squeezed fruit and mint and fizzy water is far more wonderful, far more exciting than a bunch of grapes, rotted down.

I'm not going to give you the whole story, that history of drink and alcohol.

But quickly it became a plank in my life; that thing I balanced along to keep me level.

Quickly it became the thing I waited for, till the minute hand passed across the hour so that I could pour the drink.

Quickly it became something I became anxious about if I knew I was to go an evening without.

It became my comfort blanket, my I-can-speak-to-people-trumpet, my I-can-go-to-sleep-cloak, my balm: to relax, to smooth, to gentle, to become still.

Sometimes it convinced me that I had interesting things to say, gave

184

me the confidence to challenge and argue. At those times, if I had seen me, I would have taken me outside, put me in a bin to sober up and stop embarrassing the world with whoever I thought I was being.

I can remember the maudlin me, whining about sadness, seeking affection, saying to my dad, 'How dare you have done that!'

I remember becoming almost weepy for the sadness of an imaginary past that my dazzled brain could only just reach into. That cloying self-pity for I-know-not-what, but I thought I deserved it. I thought I deserved it so much. Thinking of that makes me sick with the self-obsession of me that even today I carry out as I tap away at this laptop. These words that, when people ask what I am writing about, I always say, 'You know me. I always write about me!'

And we giggle a tiny bit.

I keep my alcohol in my tiny utility room above the freezer and the washing machine.

I now live in a tiny house. There is a sitting room, a minute kitchen, a utility room, a boxroom, a bedroom and a bathroom that is just big enough to take a three quarter length bath.

I love my house. I would like something just that bit bigger. I expect, if I measured its area, it would be a fifth of the size of the house I lived in with my wife.

But it is mine. Well, it's not. It's the bank's but it feels like mine. I like to know I have somewhere to curl up and retreat to. Somewhere for my books, my jars of beans and packets of pasta and my utility room full of alcohol.

I collect it. I get this excitement when I see a new type of alcohol and have enough money to buy it. I don't have enough for expensive alcohol so mainly I buy value whisky. But over the years, sometimes I have malt whisky. There are a number of bottles with an inch of whisky in them that have been there for ages and ages. There are green bottles of some sort of herby thing from Zaragossa, there are bottles of pastis and brandy. And Sambuca and sherry and bottles of beer that are probably out of date because I took them from my last house.

185

As I sit here, I think again about alcohol, about what it does to me. It can be fab, it can make an evening glow.

I have resisted what people tell me. Occasionally I have seen an addictions CPN but they have been very uninspiring and not particularly sure why they are seeing me, it seems. When I have been admitted to hospital, I have been put on some drug, I can't remember why. Something to do with vitamins and something about precautions to stop me fitting when I suddenly stop drinking.

I don't know why. I never have any problem when I know I can't drink. If I know that I won't be drinking for a night or a week or a month then there is never a problem. It is when I don't know if I will or won't get a drink that the problems occur.

When I have been in hospital I automatically lose my driving licence because of being diagnosed as psychotic. Trying to travel the Highlands by public transport to do my job is pretty difficult. Meetings that I would have left at ten for and got back at five from, I have to get up at five in the morning and don't return until nine in the evening.

I last lost my driving license because my GP told the DVLA that I drank too much and was mentally ill too. My psychiatrist and CPN, who are the people I see most, didn't agree. However, I lost my license for six months. Well, by the time it was all done, for nine months.

Even more yucky and embarrassing; even if the real professionals did say I wasn't addicted to alcohol, wasn't dependent on it, didn't drive over the limit.

But there is that nagging doubt at the back of my head that says, 'If you didn't drink so much she would never have thought of filling those forms in the way she did.'

I've been thinking about alcohol and my partnership with it. I think last night I went to bed early because I was muzzy, because I was aware of a faint slur in my words and a lack of capability to carry on the conversation with the people I had invited over for dinner without embarrassing myself, and the early knowledge that I didn't want to stay downstairs without more to drink and that if I drank more I would have a hangover in the morning.

I woke at 4.30 and at last, after many years, I know part of the reason that I sometimes only get three hours or so sleep a night is because alcohol is useless for sleep. People like me use it to escape into sleep and yet it does the opposite.

I use alcohol to not be.

I use it to get rid of the silence.

I used to say I use it to stop thinking, to find oblivion. And I do. I use it so that I don't have to face myself. So that I can switch off. Not be. Not be me.

But today, as I stare at the blue autumn sky and try to understand why I am writing this, try to understand what I am trying to convey and what I want to say. What I want to say and who I want to say it to and why I am doing this.

Today I think, as I contemplate; I think I take a drink to find myself sleepy by nine. That I do it, not because I can't face thinking, but because when I look at myself I find nothing there.

I find when I look at myself, that the soul of us that we treasure so much, that core, that identity, that purpose. That basic reality is not there.

If I said I do not exist you would say, 'Oh he's getting ill again!'

But if I say I have made so many layers, coated myself with so many identities, made a skintight coat of armour of me, with my work, my illness, my different roles, become so anxious and scared of enjoying myself that there's just nothing much there, would that make sense?

I cannot see me. I do not identify with me. I think I drink to hide from that, to hide from the void inside me. I think that although I poke and prod and rummage around in my memories, I just cannot find me.

I think I drink to hide from this. This emptiness.

I have just listened to a politician on the radio and I thought, *He is like that. He is so empty and so concerned for how he should be seen, and for all the causes he wants to believe in, that everything he does seems made up, seems manufactured, seems false.* I would not like him governing our country.

How can a man who has no idea who he is govern us?

I am like that too. I have no idea who I am. I can dissect me, pull me to pieces, but out of those pieces you won't find me.

187

So when I am weary and sleepy and muzzy and swirling with alcohol, I can forget that I am not me.

I can forget that I am made of cardboard.

And now that I know that I am made of cardboard, now that I see my terror of being me, I need and I don't know how; I need to find that me that I am comfortable with, that me who doesn't try to obliterate me in order to get through the night.

Wouldn't it be wonderful if I could spend an evening not only not drinking but not even wishing to drink! Ah, yes. All these steps to take. I am not sure I am ready for them. As I tell my friends, I am not even an adult yet. I haven't left adolescence so how on earth do I take on all these responsible decisions?

MOONLIGHT

It is some time since I have seen the moonlight. In the summer the sky was dark late and the sun got up early, and luckily for me I tended to sleep through the middle bit.

I have a hankering for something different. I would like to wander along the flat of a moor under the mountains and look around me on the night of a bright full moon. It would be good to see the stars and to look at the ground covered in a pale wash of moonlight. I would like that faint shudder of worry as a bird, maybe an owl, flits past in the dark or the white blur of a sheep suddenly dashes across the heather. Or from the road, a car's headlights catches the shine of a deer's gaze, standing stock still in the dark.

And then I would like to find a rock by a small lochan. I would sit beside it, feeling the cold stone through the cloth of my trousers, watching the slight spangle of ripples on the water, the silver tracery and the black lines of the dark water; maybe a moth would flap past my face. In previous years I would have smoked a cigarette, watched the brief flare and sudden darkness. Now I would hope that I could sit patiently, listening to my breath going in and out, hearing the lightest of splashes as the small ripples reached shore, feeling a wisp of breeze on my face and slowly, slowly, calling forth memories and histories.

Letting myself drift, thinking of times of happiness and times of joy and the odd hint of the memory of melancholy. Remembering the feel of fingertips on me and the clutch of small hands in my larger one; remembering laughter, remembering small times like doing the washing up together and all the laughter it involves; remembering present times when we cuddle on the sofa or water the flowers.

And then sitting up, standing up stiffly and walking along the heather-bound path besides a stream, under the crags and back to the house by the sea for coffee and music and musing before the dawn breaks.

WALKING SONGS

I spend a lot of time walking, walking alone, and in this solitariness I find peace of a sort.

Sometimes I walk with Anne or Mhairi or Sarah or Jean, but mainly I walk alone.

There is something about the beach at low tide. That sweep of sand stretching way, way down to the sea, the silver gleam of the pools of water, the sparkling diamonds where the sea sits in between the rippled sand. And always the crows and the oyster catchers and the gulls, the sandpipers and the ducks and geese. I love the sound they make. I love the way they sit at the shore line or bob silently just offshore.

There are the sandcasts of the shellfish and the worms, the mussels and razor shells, the whelks and the cockles. Bits of the beach are smooth and firm to walk on while at other places your feet sink deep into the sand and the sweat breaks out on your back.

When the tide is far, far out I sometimes walk way along below the river mouth, alongside the muddy sandy banks where there are stones and weeds and dead crabs. At other times I walk along the salt marsh by Culbin forest avoiding those muddy bits too.

I have always promised myself to walk to Findhorn bay one day but I never do. In fact I rarely reach Culbin. Somehow, in recent years, I have become more and more unfit; even climbing a slight hill makes me run out of puff.

I think my favourite time is when the wind is blowing and the dry sand is blown along the beach, pattering against my trousers and shoes. It really is like smoke across the sand, or veils of whiteness cloaking the beach, and when you peer down, all those granules hissing as they are blown along.

When you are facing the wind, your eyes tear and your face goes tight with the cold and, if it is very windy, you have to turn your back to the wind to stop the sand getting in your eyes.

I also like those cold wintry days, when the beach glistens and the rain showers cover the Black Isle and those days when all you want to do is lie back against a sand dune and soak up the sun.

I think as I walk. I go all over the place and often I get mournful, but somehow it feels when I am walking that I am free to let my thoughts in, to let them in safely, surrounded by the wide world, the sun, the sea, the high clouds.

As I walk along, my thoughts calm, somehow my movement and the openness allow them to shoogle around until they settle in smoother strands. Something peaceful; so different to a sweat-filled night when I am assaulted by these same thoughts.

All these walks over the last four years… Along beaches, through forests and beside rivers. Trying to make sense of my life, trying to overcome the loneliness, trying to see why I might have to get my jag. Or trying to make sense of a world that is so uncertain to me that I do not even understand myself a tiny bit, cannot slot myself into any category. If I cannot make sense of me, what can those around me see in me?

It's strange that, weekly or bi-weekly, I have seen my CPN over the past four years and it is odd and a bit sad that I do not really know what we have talked of. That I cannot see how I have changed. That I cannot see that life has become lighter and much brighter. I do now have more of an energy, almost a hope of something. I do believe that I can make friends and even that I do have friends. Somehow there are parts of my life that are not as empty and arid as I sometimes think they are.

I would not put it all down to my CPN, but she has been a reassuring presence. She is there to talk to, to talk to when the thoughts get too bad and what I really am looms so large.

I don't know what it is; I can hardly put my finger on it. My CPN was there for me when someone said I was a bad manager and would not speak to me; she was there when I just could not see anything to look forward to at all; she was there for a crisis at work and when a close friend stopped talking to me; and when I hoped, each morning, that I would be run over or crash or just somehow stop. She has been there for all those occasions that we are ashamed to admit to: those times when I force myself to gatherings of my friends and acquaintances, those times when I would smile and smile in my heart but feel so worried, so confused about how to speak and so confused about what to speak about.

But she has also been there as, over the years, I have made real new friends; to celebrate my awakening to the knowledge that some people can like me. She was there to hear me bubbling over with the joy I feel at Anne's and Mark's, where we revel in silliness and then get serious in our drunkenness; there to hear how much fun I had with Charlotte and Anthea and Louise walking the Black Isle; there when I ambled around at weekends with people I work with and there when, over and over, I could and at the same time could not talk about my wife and my son.

We have developed advance statements and Wrap plans . I have signed my risk assessment sheets and crisis plans. We have been to CPA meetings and discussed the various renewals of my section.　　　We have looked at anxiety management and talked about how negativity influences my thinking, we have even talked of my childhood and my distant past. We have talked of the pressure of work and not sleeping and taking medication.

So many things, and somehow it feels like my journey is not so harsh nowadays. I am no longer terrified that I will be whisked into hospital again the moment I admit that the evil is leaching the souls of those I love. I am not opening my cabinet to stare at the razor blades. I am not thinking how I will die. I am not shaking in my mind as I walk along. My heart is less torn, my stomach is calmer. When I wake at four I do not beg for sleep to stop me thinking. Instead I welcome the knowledge that I can doze for the next four hours and know that some of my waking dreams are likely to be pleasant.

I do find it hard that I cannot thank her properly, that there is that professionalism that says this is a job and too much gratitude would be in breach of some sort of propriety.

There have been so many blips along the way in the last few years where I have felt myself falling; all alone, all confused and frightened, especially at Christmas, when I remember my wife and son so clearly. Somehow I have felt caught by her and I don't know how I have been caught, but her presence has kept me steady, kept me on my feet, kept me talking to my family, my friends, kept me from those razor blades and that darkness.

When I am bored of the beach I walk up the River Nairn, past the bridges and the echoes under them, alongside the raspberry bushes and the brambles that I sometimes pick from as I walk. I love to see the dippers and the herons; I once saw a kingfisher flashing all blue. I like to see the ripples from the fish and to hear the soft sound of the water and the more raucous sound of the crows in the Scots Pine across the river.

I like the flowers by the path and the cows in the fields and I like to listen to music as I walk. I like to sit on the bench where the river curves, where there is a pebbly beach, where the water is dark brown and the dogs splash in the shallows and people park their bikes and children try to skim stones.

There is something about sitting on a bench and not worrying about when I will be home or who will be waiting for me. There is something about taking my whisky flask with me and sitting cross-legged at the end of the harbour, reading my book, listening to my iPod; watching the sun on the water, the darkness of the river against the green of the sea, the swans patrolling the harbour mouth, strangers ambling up and down. And there is something about thinking no one will comment, no one will remark. That I can stay until two in the morning if I want or just get up and go home and go to bed. And when I get home I can watch whatever I want on tv, keep the light on as long as I want in my room and listen to the radio for as long as I want too. Considering what I am supposed to be going through, it is a remarkably easy and privileged existence. And the walks. Oh, they keep my body warm, but cool down that busy brain, make it that wee bit smoother.

October

COCKTAILS AT EIGHT

Do you remember how it all began? How my life shifted from loneliness to this? I am sitting eating breakfast, reading a book, but I have stopped reading because I am sitting, staring into nowhere and smiling.

We were standing outside the Co-op, early in the morning, a year ago, clutching a bag of sandwiches bought for our meeting in Inverness, later in the day. Both of us were sore-headed, muzzy, full of too little sleep and too much talking and too much alcohol. Though we do not know it, this is the start of our relationship. Sarah will be here in a moment after dropping the children off, but for the moment it is cold and the sky is bleak and yet somehow we manage to giggle a little about how unwise it is to drink on a working night.

The night before, I cooked for Sarah and you. I think it was the last time I was allowed to cook in her kitchen. I made so many oily splashes that ever afterwards, I was asked to carry round food that I had made in my own house. I cooked corn fritters and mango salsa and made salads. I put together a jug of tequila and lime and Cointreau for margaritas and you arrived late, but not so late that it mattered. I can't remember why you were there, some work thing, but I do not recollect what work thing.

Dinner was great, just that nattering and telling of stories. You and Sarah talked far more than me; talking of children and past relationships, of that whole confusion of living. Later, back at mine, we talked more and I can't even remember much of what we said, but at one point I remember you had fallen into a doze on the couch, prompting me to realise that my bed beckoned before the seagulls woke me with the arrival of dawn.

I first met you many years ago when you started working for VOX, our national voice in mental health. I would occasionally come to directors' meetings and in the breaks, I would sit in the corner with my headphones on, a book in my hand, ignoring everyone. Yet you would come and sit beside me, convinced I wasn't really that antisocial, but I think I was. I think in those years I was a wee bit cut off, a wee bit fragile and even now, I sometimes meet people who say that when I was at VOX meetings or speaking at conferences that I was clearly ill. I think some people wondered if it was right to have someone who was so obviously struggling, speaking out at public events. It never occurred to me to do any different, but then again, I never knew people thought I was struggling. I remember I did like it that you came and talked to me, that when we met at events we would naturally meet each other, seek each other out at coffee time.

And then a few years ago, when I was still with my wife, we were both invited to Wales to talk about our work in Scotland, in the hope that it might help with something similar there. I remember so much our incredulity at the cynicism we encountered, from people even we had heard of; their conviction that it was a waste of time, that it would all be pointless. I remember we huddled together at lunchtime wondering why they had flown us down to talk with them, why they had been commissioned to do this work; slightly incredulous, slightly scandalised.

Our flights were both delayed for ages and ages and we talked away of this and that and that and this. You witnessed an awkward call with my wife and off we went.

I had always seen you as a work colleague, just that. A work colleague that I liked well enough to ask to keep in touch if, after you had your babies, you didn't go back to work. And yet now, after our talk and our talk and our drunken talk, and you witnessing my dramatic snoring through the wall, somehow I could see something more. There was some connection, some reaching out, a chance to learn of each other in a new way.

And that, over the months, is what has happened. A slow getting to know, to text, to meet, to realise over the months that we might both be yearning for each other.

THE SHAMEFUL CUT

When I first cut myself, I thought I was about to die. That was what I wanted.

I remember that desperation; the shaking as I pulled up my sleeve and the white coldness on my skin as I unwrapped my razor blade from its paper wrapping.

And I remember night after night my loathing; my hatred that I could manage little more than a few shallow cuts. The shake in my hands when I promised myself that I would lash down violently and how each time my arm stayed itself, slowed itself down until all there was, was a shallow cut, drip-dripping, and me curled up crying because I still hadn't killed myself.

After a time I stopped believing I was trying to die and although I knew nothing of words like self- harm, I began to realise I just wanted to damage myself. That I was no longer trying to die.

Eventually, as the evenings drew by and the cold loneliness of the chair I was sitting in became too much, I would know that I would be cutting myself that night.

I would spread the newspaper below me on the floor.

I would take out the box of razor blades.

I would be bathed in that white fear and that anticipation.

I would slide the edge of the blade across my wrist.

The slight red line would fill with beads of blood.

And I would slide that blade over and over and harder and harder.

The blood would well up and slip hot and yet also cold, over my skin, until it began to patter on the paper below.

After a time the pool of blood on the paper would turn black and solidify and I would fold the newspaper up, put it in the bin and slide beneath the sheets of my bed. The actual cutting never hurt but by the time I was in bed my arm would be aching and hurting and I would hold it close to me and hope no new blood started flowing to stain the sheets. And that was how I was able to relax enough to sleep.

I would feel utterly alone and lost.

I don't know why I do it.

I have no idea why it is so important to keep a box of razor blades in my bathroom, just in case. Just in case I need to escape; just in case I cannot be; just in case I cannot cope. I do not know why I would wish to harm myself; why I am that fox in its cage. I know sometimes it has been my way of saying, 'This is how I feel,' when I cannot speak it.

I know that I have been stitched up without an anaesthetic but that there was some medical reason for doing this. I know that my first doctor said he would stop seeing me if I didn't stop cutting myself and how I was filled with a terrible fear when I couldn't, and how, after he said that, he said he was just trying to see if I could stop. I know I was told off lots of times. I know sometimes I wanted people to see what I had done.

I know I hope I never do this again and that I wish I could wipe those scars from my skin. I do not understand why I could sit for an hour in hospital rubbing the tines of a fork against my skin until a clear fluid began to gather and my hand began to sting with the sweat that got into it. And how I carried on rubbing the fork into the wound until the blood began to drip past my thumb. I do not understand. When I look at that scar on the back of my hand I feel a sense of disgust. Why do I do things like this?

I can't believe I had the willpower to stub cigarettes out on my hands. To hear a sizzle and see the ash burnt into the skin and the rise of the black blister, and feel joy that it didn't hurt so much that I couldn't do it again.

I don't understand why I took the tips off hairgrips so I could rip myself or stole pins to drag into me. How each time I am in hospital, every waking moment is about finding ways in which I can hurt myself and how, when I am in this place, all those nurses spend so much time ensuring that I don't harm myself.

I cannot understand my joy that I could pour boiling water over my fingers and my hand when in hospital, feel the shock of the burn and the relief of seeing my skin turn bright red and, over the days, turn scaly and tough and rigid and blistered until, by and by, it peeled away leaving fresh skin below.

I hate that I can do that to myself. I hate that, as I write this, I can remember the relief it gave me. That I can see me getting out of bed and going to the cupboard in the bathroom for my razor blades. I hate that if I didn't have people around me, if I didn't have my wish to be free of all of this, if I didn't know I was happy that this would be a temptation to revel in.

I hate that it is like a drink or a drug and that once I make the first cut I could carry on and on and find myself in a familiar world I want so much never to visit again.

I want that world to be a nightmare I shudder about and thank my stars I will never re-enter.

November

MAKING MEMORIES

I pinched resin from a pine tree, crumbled it in my fingers to release the vapour and, remembering you, added pine needles.

Remembering you and also he, who sold us the soap on a cold wet day in Aberfoyle. I remember you and me walking around, dripping wet, hand in hand, giggling about the sweaters and Scottish music, the shortbread and the tartan rugs.

We both remember him, sitting glum at the 'natural soap' stall, all incongruous, rolling a cigarette and telling us there was nothing doing around here, nothing to see, just nothing.

Then, when we said we might be going to the hotel along Loch Katrine for coffee, doing a double take, looking at us suspiciously and saying, 'You'll not be short of money then.'

I remember my bar of pine tree soap with the amber gleam and the coating of needles and I remember Loch Katrine and its half-submerged road. I remember the hotel where we decided we were very rich today and I ate an animal for the first time in 27 years; I remember you leaned over and kissed me while the ladies in the corner laughed and the French waiter played at being a French waiter and we decided we were sophisticated.

Now I remember when I shower and the pine needles scrape my skin; I smell the cleanness, the sharpness, feel the slippery wash. I also remember the dank, dark, green smell of the undergrowth of the forest where the light is dim but butterflies might fly in summer.

I remember you putting your hand in my pocket, feeling the bar of soap, laughing at how a man like me would spend all that money on soap and how we turned round and kissed again as we walked out the hotel lobby. And how we still turn red when we recollect the station master in Perth who chucked us out for being too affectionate, how we laugh at the glum man and how I have to pick pine needles out of my bath each time I shower.

Each time I remember and each time I shower I know I am that much closer to when I see you again, when we will laugh about our new memories, snuggle up for kisses and play dares about whether this time I will eat a fish or whether a mollusc is just enough for now; just that bit risky enough, that bit too much on the edge of an adventure.

JUST MUSING

Another very early morning sitting in the lounge of a hotel. From my couch I can see the silver-pink waters of the loch and a collection of motley but expensive cars in the car park. There are bands of dark clouds and pale orange strips of sunlight in between the eggshell blue of the sky.

Soon my parents will come downstairs and we will share our breakfasts and think about what to do for the day.

It has taken me so many years to see my parents stripped from the layers of expectation and anger with which I surrounded myself.

It is good to look on my dad with his stooped back and silver hair, to feel that faint hint of surprise each time I see the stubs of his fingers where the rope on the winch cut through skin and bone. It is something new to look on his dark tanned face and his swelling belly and to think that I like being in his company. To realise that my lack of a fluid conversation is not so much a lack as a stereotype of awkward men of a certain generation who tend to need the skills of women to be able to speak and charm and who, at other moments when alone, fall silent.

It is good to realise that sometimes we do not talk and talk, because those subjects we may talk of are ones where we know we disagree; that it is more tactful and respectful to refrain from the need for petty arguments which serve no purpose other than to alienate and diminish that bond that speaks of love and the need to constantly reach out, even when we are frightened of words and cautious with the past and our expression of emotion.

I am not too interested in seeing my dad as my father, of elevating or maybe reducing him to all that comes along with that label. I like to catch glimpses of his humour, I like to see the pleasure he takes in a glass of wine or a plate of food. I like to see him reading his Kindle and so obviously not doing the washing up after tea. I can almost feel both his pain and his humiliation as he spends time rocking back and forth when trying to get to his feet from an armchair. Or holding his leg with both hands to get his foot out the car, or getting a hold of both the car door and his walking stick before standing up. I understand his regret and I understand his thought that his life is now limited in joy and time.

And yet now, as I look out the window and see the loch lit up in a streak of orange by the sun, I understand how my mum feels at such thoughts and I want to hold her tight and say, 'Don't worry, he still loves you, still aches for you. Don't worry, this is no ending.'

I want her to know that the extraordinary beacon of love she has held for him for decades and decades still shines, still glows, that it is all worth it. That the slow decline and the difficulty of emotion does not mean that he rejects her love, her faith, her way of living. More that he is some great shaggy bear grown tired, shaking his head and nuzzling the leafy bed in his cave. That he is an old carthorse, left in the meadow to munch on the grass and press against his partner with a muzzy head and a relief that he is no longer pulling the load of the day, no longer having to battle on his back legs with his hooves flying, and at the same time hazy with regret. Wanting to be the vigorous, action-filled, anger-filled, ambition-consumed man of his younger days. Wanting that energy and zest and maybe wanting to change some of the things that energy and zest can cause you to do. Because the cautious pause to consider your actions does not always occur to you when you are filled with adventure.

I think to myself that maybe my mum would like to be looked after a bit now too; would perhaps feel happier if she wasn't responsible for everything nowadays.

And I look at her, at her red-rimmed eyes and slight body, and I think she swims faster and for longer than I can; she walks over fields and along cliffs when I am lying comatose on my couch, that it is only late in the evening that she pauses from the cooking, the cleaning, the gardening, the daily ever present task of being alive, of celebrating, of making jokes and giggling, of comforting and just getting on with life.

There is something I cannot express about her and maybe that is because I am a man who in company has few words and who hesitates in how to express them and whose perception is suspect.

She knows duty and she knows how to behave. She knows the dangers of giving up and falling silent and hopeless, but she is no wind up toy. She brims with affection and love and a dance in her spirit; a dance that says, 'Do not waste all the precious things that make up this life.'

Sometimes I think there is an incomprehension when she encounters people who have fallen silent and who, if ever they knew hope, left it far behind.

Ah, that doesn't do her justice. When I walk into her kitchen she greets me with a great big hug. When I talk on the phone, as soon as I get hesitant she will lift the conversation and I will travel along it with her. She is so funny when we tidy up and so good at wittering about the whole wide world when we walk along the cliffs, up at the 'barn walk'. And so good at making anyone, whoever they are, feel welcome and treasured in her life. I don't know how else to describe her, really.

I love that I can drive in the car with my parents and we can be filled with nonsense and banter from the moment we set off, to the time when our journey finishes and we think of what next we might do.

WIND

I want to feel a summer breeze. A soft, warm, summer evening breeze, where the light is golden and the swallows flit over the water and the flies make sparks in the setting sun. I want to lie down in it and I want to bask in it and drink something cool and refreshing. Maybe, amid the sound of dogs being taken for an evening walk or children playing in the park, I will fall asleep and the leaves will tickle my cheeks while I slumber and my hands become hot and sweaty and streaked from the grass on which I lie. And I will wake and stretch and feel all stiff and warm and sleepy, and I will smile.

And I will not wake at three in the morning before even the summer light is there and lie in bed, uncomfortable, chased by thoughts I do not want.

I want to feel a spring gale. I want to walk amidst the new buds on the trees and the snowdrops and the daffodils and feel the rush of wind on my face and the clutch of it in my clothes. I want to feel that wonderful joy at the spinning clouds and the waving branches. I want to look out to sea and see the waves in ranked but chaotic seahorses and I want to hold my love's hand and run across the sand.

And I will not sit in my car in the evening, staring at the road in the gathering dusk, chased by thoughts I do not want.

I want to feel an autumn haze with rain and wood smoke. It would be good to see cattle walking through the fields, to hear the tractors and see the bales of hay. It would be good to watch the red and yellow, the brown and blackened leaves spiral to the ground. I would watch the geese flying in their wide 'V's overhead and I would listen to the sound they make, which makes me wistful and calm and peaceful.

And I will not stare at the telly in the evening, drowning out the noise of my thoughts with the chatter of comedy programs.

I want to feel the winter cold and the dryness in the air and the crackle of frost around my face. I would love to watch the sun making the trees black and golden in the evening and listen to the chatter of my love's bright-faced children as they walk through the forest walk, clutching their soft toys to them; making up stories that burst with newness and the ancient wisdom of innocence.

And I will not work late on my computer, clicking through emails, chasing away the thoughts I do not want.

FREEDOM

Today they were deciding on whether to recommend renewing my section again. Sometimes I just get so fed up with all of this. So fed up and angry. I am called for my care programme approach meeting and then not called for it and then called for it after all, by which time my car is in the garage and my named person is a day's journey away when she had previously booked the time off. It just feels like they cannot care. And yet I know they do. In a way.

But I work. My named person works. I have things to do. I do not like being juggled around because someone, somewhere, has made mistakes with schedules. I do not like the fact that I have to travel for three and half hours, cover only thirty miles, to attend a meeting I didn't want to go to.

I hate co-operating; being honest and open and friendly and sharing a laugh. It is my freedom you are discussing and taking notes on. I know the arguments. I do know them. I am furious.

What are the conditions for my section? You almost tap them off your fingers; we are so used to this debate. I have schizophrenia. So I have a mental illness. Well, *I* know I don't, it just looks like I do. I don't feel ill. I don't feel different. I am me. That is all. I am me. You are saying I am ill because I am me.

I benefit from treatment. There is nothing to treat, there just isn't, and yet I can neither explain this to myself or to you. My CPN, what she does is great, it is all anyone would want – those warm and wise conversations and that wonderful support when I find the world difficult. Everyone should have someone close to them like that who they can confide and share stories with.

I know, I know so well those days when we went through my hospital notes, all those points you made, see?

'You stopped taking medication then and then and then and not long after you were in hospital.'

And I know, I know. I even know and remember that at the time I said, 'I cannot argue with that, my diagnosis must be right.'

I cannot explain to you why it is wrong. I get myself all tangled up. It isn't right. Somewhere this has all gone wrong but I am not sure how, and I am sure that I am not ill . Sometimes I just yearn to be me. Living a false life seems so wrong and taking this drug that hides my evil from me, how can I agree to that? All these years of breathing badnesss into the air, poisoning the joy that can fill life and just not seeing it because the drugs disguise the reality. And I dread more than anything those times when I really know how bad I am. But this pretence that I am not so awful, how can we let that slip by unnoticed? We must one day confront what I am and deal with it.

Yet sometimes I don't think this. I think to myself that the medication is just some sort of placebo, that if it were changed to saline solution I would just carry plodding along not getting 'ill', not doing anything much, and at other times I worry that it *is* poison we slip under my skin every two weeks. But mostly I just know it is so wrong for me to take medication. I need to be real again, how on earth can we want for anything else?

I am at risk. And I just don't think I am. I just don't think I am. You, my psychiatrist, say I get ill quickly. That I want to set fire to myself without the jags; that I want to drain the evil away. And I know I do. But maybe, just once, I could live free; live with a joy in myself; live not thinking about evil. Maybe I will not always be that way. Maybe I could take that chance?

And my judgement is impaired. I am making sense now! I am seeing your point. I know your arguments, I realise that it might be right, it might be true that I have an illness. Being evil might be a delusion. I know you might be right and me wrong, that all these things might be symptoms of an illness. Doesn't the fact that I can see this, mean that my judgement is not impaired? Doesn't the fact that I know I might have impaired judgement almost mean that I can't have impaired judgement?

217

Doesn't it? The fact that I am almost as frightened as you all are of the day when I can be free and stop that medication, that jag. This must mean that I know what I am doing. Sort of?

I want to walk in the clouds where no one ever looks at me again. I don't want this to be happening. I don't want my life to be this way.

I don't want to have to say how angry I am with my obtuseness, my refusal to accept what everyone says. I want to go right back to the beginning and make none of this happen. I want to be a stockbroker with three children and a Labrador.

I don't want to humiliate myself any more with the stories that I have to tell the tribunals, where they look at me with kindly faces and dismiss what I say.

I don't want to be in that bulging file of notes that you carry around with you. And I don't want to be unusual. And I don't want to be summoned at a moment's notice to my tribunal. My tribunal where I will be stared at and studied and decided about. Where even I will be frightened about what will happen if I win. And I don't want to make jokes when I am miserable. And I don't want to be intense and I don't want to be here.

And I know you phoned my named person on your day off and I know you will work over Christmas and that you will do it to keep me safe.

I know all of this. I know every single little scrap of all of this. I want to curl up. I don't want to speak.

I hate mental illness. I hate every element of it. I don't want to go for my jag tomorrow. I don't want to sit in the waiting room, wondering how much it will hurt. I don't want to take my antidepressants. I want to be free of all of this. I want to cover my eyes and scream and I want to say, 'I don't see you, I don't know you. I don't know who you are, I don't recognise you.

And then I want to whisper that I don't know what I am and I want to whisper, 'Someone put their arms round me and hold me and let me know how to feel again.'

December

WINTER OUTSIDE MY WINDOW

I am circling the winter, watching out for those blue days with dried leaves edged with frost and hopefully somewhere, a plume of smoke rising from a house on the edge of a stubble field. I am looking for icicles and grasses and mosses frozen in clumps. And mounds at the edge of streams where the stones in the middle gleam with a white cap of snow. I am standing looking across a stream towards the humped bridge at the end of the field. Remembering.

And somewhere I am learning, learning to speak, learning to leave silence for those short intervals where I regain space from all those people I now know. I am learning the benefits of a walk in a field, swinging our clasped hands wildly back and forth. I am learning how to judge how wet a park seat will be for the small spaces when the children do not demand our company, while they sail the pirate ship away, away, from the red and green spider machine in the field.

I have a vision of a snow field, up beyond Ryvorn bothy, where the snow rises in plumes in the bright windy sky. The sound of my skis swishing, the sound of my laboured breathing and the heat of me under all the layers combine to make me both anxious and exhilarated. And my vision is a memory of a winter a long, long time ago, probably not to be repeated. But I am sure that the snowballs you will throw at me, the wee icy trickle down my back from the children's play will be very real indeed and I hope that I will learn to laugh at that, to gambol; puffing, laughing, hiding the natural scowl my face always reverts to.

I can hear the sound of the flume banging in the wild gale of the wind and the scattered battering of rain across my window. I can see the orange glow of the night through my curtains, hear the rapid clatter of a can rushing along the road outside and the sudden bang as the lid of the bin outside is blown open. And I am not lonely, I am not wondering about my future. Instead, I am looking forward to the time when you will text to say you are free to talk. That the children are asleep and you have tidied away the day and can now tell me all about the wildness of the Clyde outside your own window.

I am wondering about the forecast, seeing snow swirling in the street lights. Thinking that if it is snowing down here by the Firth then, on the drive across the country, the roads will be blurred; the tyre tracks almost lonely in the silence. And as I wonder about this and the wisdom of setting off for work, it occurs to me that I do not have to set off, do not need to drive myself ever onwards; that I can text you to say how lucky I am to spend a day working from home.

The sea is heaving itself over the harbour wall in great gouts. The path has crumbled along the promenade and up river the water has spread across The Maggot, covering the path, lapping up against the small flood defences at the entries to the lanes besides Fishertown. I am again feeling glad that my house is slightly raised above the river; that it is probably beyond reach of any normal flood. I am taking photos to post on Facebook, to tag you in, with some query about your own home, way up on the side of the hill.

When the dusk closes in on us in mid afternoon, I want to tell you all about it. I want to tell you about everything. I want to learn to talk, I want to escape from the gloom and sit in a warm room, drinking tea, wittering. Yes, me. Wittering. I am learning to witter… and to smile.

A CHRISTMAS CAROL

I cannot stand Christmas music. I hate it. Meaningless, saccharine songs about greed. A disgusting welter of self satisfaction. The worst, I think, are the ones about world aid or peace and times of plenty. I am not a good judge of English but even to me the lyrics of the songs are cloying and repugnant. And the way they are sung! As if Christmas were the most amazing wonderful thing that ever happened, as though a week of getting drunk and eating too much is all we ever looked forward to in our lives.

I hate this time of year and I don't really know why. Ever since I left my wife, and maybe before, I have hated it. I don't like the staff Christmas lunches and I don't know how to relax and have fun. I don't like how I feel; that sleeplessness, that nagging feeling of anxiety and sadness tugging at my stomach and my throat. That wish to find somewhere far away to curl up and sleep and not, not, not think.

This year, after all the years of refusing to, I have gone down to visit my parents. All those years, where being with my family at Christmas filled me with a dread I couldn't explain. A dread of not only having to perform, to be happy, but also feeling I have to answer for my own fractured family and that dread of never being alone and quiet.

A dread of Santa Claus on telly and more Christmas songs and getting too cheerfully drunk, day after day. And yet now I am here, I am, in a way, very happy.

Sitting downstairs with the curtains drawn, the night pitch black outside while I type. My eyes a wee bit red raw with tiredness and a wee bit raw from driving for hours and hours and a wee bit red from drinking till midnight. I feel a bit peaceful.

My parents are staying up the road so that we can all fit in the house and yet I feel a different regret and a kind of shame.

My wife never liked my sister or brother or their partners. Never liked my parents. And I don't know. At one time I hated my parents too.

But I think I let it drag on and never looked around me, never thought about it. I let that informal estrangement be. Knew my family were awkward about visiting us because we were awkward with them. I knew my wife hated those visits and just let it be.

Since then. Since I left, amid those accusations of how I was turning into my dad, was just like him in all the worst ways, I have been phoning my parents. Talking away, getting used to each other, getting used to the fact that if it is Sunday and eight o'clock and I haven't phoned, my parents will be wondering what is happening. And that I look forward to those calls so much.

I am also getting used to the fact that when I phone my sister, we may speak for ages and ages and yet if we phone and one or the other of us is in our formal mode, we will not speak for long.

Getting used to the hums and ha's of my brother when he phones; how he is nearly always cooking when I speak and how he is glad to speak and yet how he can be as out of place on the phone as a duck landing on ice.

It was strange, yesterday, to listen to Sharon talk about how it felt when my wife made her cry when she was telling her off for being a doctor and sad to hear of other estranged families. And there was an ache in me. A huge ache when I looked at my brother, who was pretending he liked his brand new beard, pretending to be grumpy at his children's derision of it.

I did not know what I missed all those years when we saw my family just for duty visits. Jenny, my niece, is almost grown up and going out with boyfriends; arguing with her mum and dad about the length of her skirt and whether she will wear tights or not to the party. Harry is getting bigger and reminds me all the time of my son, though maybe with less of an edge. Louise is being a teenager, being clever, doing things with iPads. All of them looking devastatingly beautiful or handsome. And why do I also know so little of Fergus and Keli, of Andrew and Eileidh and Thomas?

And I think, *But I am with my family now.*

And last night, again finding out new things, hearing about the conversation my brother had with one of my psychiatrists, the last time I was in hospital. The one who said he wanted to take me off all my medication and keep me in hospital for a year to find out what was really going on with me. To find out that my brother gently had to explain to him that if he did that just to find out, that I would lose my job, lose my house, lose my possessions. That maybe, although it would be good to find out what goes on, they needed to think of my life too. Another wee bit of information I just didn't know about.

And a new thought in my head that maybe the doctors don't think I am ill either, that maybe how they define me is looser than they say.

And my sister. Why didn't my wife like her? I think my family was the setting for some sort of drama of class war. Of insecurity and prejudice and the war, where resentments and anger over how people have behaved, especially my dad, were not set aside but were allowed to fester and grow and become monsters.

Now, as I sit here in the early morning, I think, *They were my family. Why did I neglect them? Why did I grow distant? Why didn't I share their adulthood and their dramas and their births and their hopes and their worries?*

Why did I do that?

My brother. Whose room I shared for so many years. Whose Action Man I tore in two. Whose tears I watched at school. My brother, with whom I shared my childhood. My sister, who was born on the same day as me and who I was told was my birthday present. My sister, who we would run with, each of us holding her arms high so that her feet were just skipping on the sand and she would be laughing with us so much. My sister who is full of ideas, who doubts herself almost as much as me, who runs shiatsu classes for pregnant mothers, who visits the Goddess Temple in Glastonbury. My sister, who last night celebrated the solstice in a yurt in a wild storm with a group of women, doing and saying things I will never understand.

My dad, my mum. The people who made me, brought me up. Worried about me. Loved me even when I thought they didn't.

What have I done?

I am in a room full of memories. There are photos of the jet fighters my dad flew and the ocean racing yachts he sailed on. There is the picture of the house by the water that I always loved looking at, always wanted to visit. There are wedding photos and photos of children and the sofas that we have sat on for decades. There are even the teaspoons that some aunt who taught in Japan way, way, back in the early 1900s brought back and which ended up with my mum. There are the CDs we try to avoid listening to. There is the drinks cabinet with bottles that Richard and I took secret sips from when we were little.

This is my history. This is my family. This is what I tried to escape from and this is what was always there for me. Always there although I didn't know and didn't want and shouted and scowled at.

This is wonderful, yet still I am sad and still I hate Christmas and still I think of my son. Still I think, *Will he one day sit in my house and look at his history?*

I suppose not. There is nothing in my house that he grew up with, nothing that belonged to him. He has never seen my house and I think he no longer has an interest in my parents' house or the houses of his cousins on this side of the family.

We are fractured and I have gone home and I am still welcome, as I must have known I would be.

In the dark of this early morning I hear the sound of the rain on the windows of this house that once was my home. My mum, sleeping in her sleeping bag on the couch in the sitting room. Hoping that the sound of my typing will not wake her. Listening to the sound of the wind in the trees and wondering if any of the last hundred or so pages I have written make sense.

I still do not understand what I am or what I have done. I know that as I sit here so early on Christmas morning that my sister's children are not even stirring in bed yet, in anticipation of opening their stockings. I know that my wife may be stirring in her bed somewhere far away, and I do not know the emotion she will wake to but I remember the last text she sent me. The text where she said I had destroyed her life. I remember the text where she asked me to tell all my family to stop asking her for my son's address because he would not want her to tell them and I sit here and think about how we can almost casually drift into worlds where all we are is some whirlwind of destruction.

If ever I wanted some confirmation that I am the devil, that I ooze evil, this effect that I have had on my small family must do that, must show that underneath the smile and the openness is that pit of evil that reeks along the dark recesses of my backbone.

And yet I take my drugs. Well, I am injected with my drugs and somehow I am told that they stop this reality.

I do not understand how you can stop, with the slip and slide of chemicals, something as basic as the nature of good and bad, the manifestation of evil and yet somehow, somewhere in the back of my heart, I think to myself that that knowledge of evil is, for the moment, a pale glimmer. I am not being shadowed to stop me killing myself and even though I know what I am, I am not filling the petrol can and lighting the match.

I do not know. I do not know whether this is a good thing. For me, the joy of gaining the ability and the chance to grow those bonds with my family and my friends, the soft warmth when people praise the meal I have made or smile fondly about me even though I am sitting in the next room with a scowl on my face and a drink in my hand. This is so wonderful.

This chance to start to live again. To cast away the world of my desperation and my set-apartness and my anger and to find ways of giving gifts of my love to those around me. It seems to me that I am so, so, lucky.

It seems to me that if this sharp needle stops me knowing how terrible I really am, that I should take that chance. I should start again, even if it is terribly selfish, even if it means the poison of my presence leaks constantly around me.

And I don't know why but I want that chance to start. To dream, to love, to dare to think of something other than despair and those relentless long days of work that mean I am free of the burden of thinking.

229

It seems to me that, somehow, I should find some way of agreeing to that fortnightly injection. That, as my brother says, I should agree to take responsibility for my medication and my health. I can't at the moment. I cannot, even though I know.

I cannot agree to that sharp jag, that recognition, that shift in awareness. But I can begin to start to think about it. I can begin to start.

I can look outside the chains I placed in my mind and I can look outside the chains I have placed around those that love me. I can look beyond that red raw wound of hurt that so many people around me wear as the burden of the consequence of loving me and I can start to learn to try to live.

I can acknowledge my tiredness and my sadness and my confusion, my role in that vicious destruction of the dream I helped my family believe in and then took away. And I can acknowledge that it is not repairable and nor do I want to repair it, but that if ever my wife or my son come to me to bear witness to what I am and what I have done, I can listen and if ever my friends and acquaintances wish to sit with me and force my heart to acknowledge what I have done to them, I can listen to them too.

But all along the way, as we approach the start of a new year, I can listen to my heart that is begging me to finally let me forgive myself and to love myself and to learn to realise that although I am way, way, into the maturity of my life that I can start.

I can start to breath and to smile and, as I start to acknowledge myself, I can start to recognise the pale strands of the webs of connection with the world that are spread all around me. And I can tug on them, reach out to them and pull myself to my feet with them and begin to wipe the detritus of so many decades from my eyes.

Mine will be the struggle that every single person lives daily and there is no reason why the struggle should have an outcome, and there is no reason that the struggle will make me or the world better; there is no goal in sight with which people will clap their hands at the end of this book and say, 'Why, he has recovered. He has won through. How sweet and how inspiring!'

230

Because that was never the point and shouldn't be. That is meaningless.

The point is learning how to be alive, how to breath, how to love and how to trust. How to work, run, sleep, run out of puff, walk on the beach, cry in the night, eat, day in and day out; work, love, trust. To learn the nature of a smile and the pain of rejection. To learn how to reject. To learn how to be alive and to know I will fail at it and that by tonight I will be bleary with alcohol and no doubt sulking again with the weight of a life built on tiredness and anxiety and resentment.

To know that when I go upstairs to the room that used to be set aside for my brother and I, I will find my love sitting inside, ready to tease me about my anxiety and ready to bring a smile to my lips and a laugh at the rebuke I always give to my life. I will put my arms around her and she will also relax and I will find that I too, can help people to start again.

GOING UNDERGROUND

Right in the middle, the light of the entrance is just a brief speck, a brightness admittedly, but vanishing, casting almost no light.

As we approach, we are giggling, searching for some sign of the exit and, of course, as everyone does, we are talking about the murderers who must lurk in the dips and the crannies of the tunnel's sides. It causes Wendy to clutch my hand just that little bit tighter, just as my hand is pretending not to do the same to hers.

This feels so exciting. I think it was Wendy who thought of it when we were searching for somewhere to stay midway between Nairn and Cardross. A hotel at the side of a busy but winding wooded road near Perth and, up on the hill, the old abandoned railway with its cuttings and its tunnels dipping into the dark of the slope.

We get lost to begin with, clambering through brambles, up muddy banks. Me, trying to be good at navigating. Wendy, trying to be impressed. Holding hands and getting sweaty in our climb, walking between puddles and muddy patches on the old tracks and then entering the tunnel, past an old couch, past rubbish, saying, 'Do we dare? Do we dare?'

And we don't even have a torch. Well, we do, but it is a very weak and feeble one.

The ground underneath is a mixture of dry, soft earth alternating with stretches of rocks and pebbles and the occasional expanse of water.

In the evening we linger over dinner, are delighted by the waiter giving us a free drink with our coffee. I love the wittering we do. We are planning the bar and restaurant that we will build there. A theme of a train going nowhere with hints of murder and the Orient. Plush seats and tables, cocktails and wine. We get lost in how to ventilate a kitchen when it's built in the middle of a hill, become worried that we would asphyxiate the guests.

Earlier in the year we went to stay with my sister and her family at friends in Traquair, near Peebles, and we had the same adventure again. Wandering alongside the river with her children or at least, some of them. Dashing all over the place, climbing trees, seeming to fall in the water, finding castles. I have a photo of Wendy and the children outlined in the tunnel entrance there, too. A slight tracery of brickwork made silver by the light and the black shapes of the people in the midst of the white arch of light.

That was a wonderful weekend. Hearing stories; a great crowd of us eating, playing games, hearing other people's histories. I think, due to space issues, we slept in the attic that night, in one of the offspring's beds. Slightly wobbly after climbing the steep ladder to the loft, slightly worried we might fall through the trapdoor if we moved too far from the bed.

We didn't of course. Breakfast was blurry, coffee welcome. The fresh air and the walk amongst the rhododendrons on the estate, a shaky but effective way of blowing the cobwebs of sleep and muzziness away. The children getting us lost in the maze by the castle. A reminder that adventures like these make life sparkly: children, tunnels, sisters, hotels, Wendy. That dark apprehension when the light is fading below the ground, just a brief thrill of delighted fear. All the more reason to hug Wendy tight, to share a cuddle, a kiss, to look forward to the next adventure. To think there might be tunnels down here in the dark of winter at Christmas.

BEING PETULANT

I asked my sister what I was like as a teenager and she said that I never spoke and was very angry all the time. That I drew dark pictures which I put on my bedroom walls.

I asked my brother what I was like and he said I was very, very quiet. That I was angry. That maybe I was justified at first in how I treated my dad, but that I took it too far. Far too far.

And soon I will ask my mum and my dad and I know what they will say.

At long, long last I know that I wasn't the person I dreamed of being. I was the typical sullen withdrawn teenager. The one who sulked and smoked out the window at night. The one ready to flare into arguments, the one blind to what went on around him. The one who kept to his room and thought, I no longer know what thoughts.

And I think, *Maybe that is what I was, always. Maybe that is what I still am. Even at the age of over fifty, I can sulk like a seventeen-year-old and be blind that this might upset others.*

I think, *People are remarkably forgiving, even when I am grumping and scowling, they are saying nice things about me, giving me hugs and touches on the arm and the chance to rejoin everyone again when I have got over myself.*

It has also occurred to me that I have followed such a typical pattern. How often are people who are later diagnosed with schizophrenia those people who withdraw, get lost in themselves, have no friends, do not communicate?

I am still struggling with this, even after all these months of writing and all these years of being me and even after this past year with Wendy, learning new ways of seeing and thinking. I look at the child who lost himself, got lost in a world he couldn't explain. I look at the young man harming himself, isolating himself. I look at the 'delusions' and I look at the times when I think people know my thoughts. At the times when I am stressed and I hear voices and don't sleep. I look at my emptiness, my despair at not feeling my emotions. I look at my blankness, my numbness, my inability to socialise. My sadness, my... Oh, I lose sight of all those things... All that horribleness.

I look at all this and I look at the times I have been in hospital.

I even remember the BBC World Service programme, early this morning, that said there is research that says people with schizophrenia have no sense of rhythm and I think, *Well that's me too – rhythm, beat. All that stuff is absolutely alien to me.*

But when I look at that sheet of paper that has schizophrenia written all over it. When I hold the tracing up, I don't see me. I see someone else.

I am bewildered. It feels made up. It feels like a mistake. It feels wrong. That is not who I am, that is not who I am.

I do not know why this is the way it is. I don't know why I am so good at getting angry at life and I don't know why I am so good at hating myself. I don't know why, when my love tells me that when I am not present, my family talks about me so lovingly, I don't understand.

I don't know why my dad is so full of admiration for me when I cannot see anything good about me.

I don't know why people can like me when I want to curl up and stop thinking for ever and ever. I do not understand and I am tired of it.

I have no idea why I want to understand.

January

PRAYING FOR A GOODBYE, SAYING HELLO

I pray the light will hold, will hold tight to my eyes even though the day is dark and the night darker still. I pray that when I sway and think of those things I don't want to, I can walk round the corner and be greeted by a great dazzle of sunlight that makes me screw up my eyes, hold my hands to my face and dance an awkward shuffle that turns into a smile.

I pray I forget my wife and yet I pray that I remember every hair on her head. I pray that I won't recognise her in the street and yet that I can replay every conversation we have ever had.

I pray that I can speak and that when I can speak that it is the truth, or at least my version of the truth and that that truth is respected. I also pray that I can hold my lips silent, hold my anger and hurt in check, keep her from my truth that she has never seen. My truth which I still hold to and which I will still speak about, though I want to protect her from it still.

I pray for peace, and that stillness that says forgiveness and regret and blame have no meaning at all when you are in that blue circle of silence. I pray that I can be and not put any emphasis on being me.

I pray that I don't have any need to pray, or to live in a place where life is so, so clear and peaceful and conclusive. And so devoid of bitterness that there is no need to preach or hope or gather myself for a better fairer world. There is just a world where I am just living, learning to laugh without expectation, learning how to talk and to smile and to cry too. To scream and to laugh and dance on the beach. Knowing it means nothing, asks nothing, just is that small movement that says, 'Here I am, doing what I do.'

Without needing either myself or anyone else to interpret my actions as anything other than a smile or indeed tears and a ruffled sleep.

I pray so much in my new life with Wendy, so much that I ache at night with it. I pray that even when I am wrinkled and my lips dribble, that though a kiss may be a wee bit off, reaching out to hold your hand with my paper-skinned fingers will bring a smile to our faces. I pray that with small words we will remember these months where we speak for hours on the phone, where we send sentimental texts of missing each other, and where we do not care that staring into each other's eyes or kissing in the middle of the street will bring a slight edge of derision to the onlooking passers-by.

And I pray that I remain full of the need to speak and natter and be silly, and to lose my heavy gravity and my calm and my patience and my being steady with the world.

I pray that I leap over traffic bollards and blow bubbles with bubble gum and ignore the glances that look askance at a man of fifty acting like a teenager.

And finally, I wish to live slightly and softly. I want to learn not to change the world and I want to learn not to be remembered and I want to learn not to be praised or thanked. I want to be the man in the pub everyone knows slightly, with an edge of slight affection. That's what I am aiming at; the ambition to be ordinary and normal and even more boring than I am already.

But before that I need to appear on television and be so outrageous and funny and moving and clever that I gain the privilege of walking down the street trying to avoid the people who recognise me and want to talk to me.

I pray for the wisdom to be immature.

STARTING TO SMILE

It is Hogmanay. I have been painting my bedroom, getting rid of the brown, getting rid of the stains. Later, I will clean the house, scrub the grout in the bathroom, clean the floors, tidy the shelves and the cupboards, sort my papers. Just show some respect to this house, this year, the future; the idea it may not be mine soon.

Then tomorrow, when I am still tidying, the year will start again and I will try to open my eyes to the world I am ambling through and make my own new start. Something of a start. Something special.

Tonight I will phone Wendy early in the evening and we will talk, maybe we will talk all the way until the bells or maybe we will slow down and take to our beds and sleep through the joining of the years together. We will talk about all sorts of things.

We will talk about whether we can really believe in having a baby and at the same time we will be checking we do want to make a commitment to each other. We will be talking about me leaving my job to come down to live with her and whether I will really get on with her children and her mixed emotions about falling in love with me so soon after stopping loving her husband.

Each thing we talk of will be something new in our lives, each decision will change both of our lives.

Coming back home to my house has made me think. It has made me realise that although I want more than anything to be able to talk in that smooth excited flow of conversation with my dad, that I still do not know how to. There is the weight of an outdated history obscuring our relationship. Having spent year on year adding stones to the scales I now need to start taking them away. I need to start taking responsibility for my feelings and know that, in my heart, there is a road of love and security that I can, and have, walked along without pausing to think or worry about and somehow, some way, that is very special to me.

When we drove back up to home we stopped at John's in the Lake District and it was very good indeed. It is funny watching John kneading dough, making flatbreads to dip in oil and then in some spicy nut mixture and to eat some wonderful concoction of bread and mushroom and cheese and some sort of sauce.

For me to be free enough and happy enough, with what almost seems like a new family, to dance to some Xbox dance thing despite my abject horror at doing so. To giggle and laugh and be ever so, ever so silly when we played poker, so silly that I think Jenny told me to shut up and I felt so warm that it didn't worry me.

I am very, very thankful that I have such people who will always welcome me and that I can bask in a warmth I didn't know existed in the way I now do.

We did speak, Wendy and I. Around about 10 pm or so, I phoned her and I do not know what we talked about but at some point while I was lying in bed, wittering with her, I heard the sound of fireworks and we both realised that we had spoken until the bells had gone, even though we had grumped and said that we wanted to sleep away through into the New Year. And so we shared a kiss on the phone and this brand New Year began.

It sounds like a nice beginning. I could quite get used to this. I could quite get used to the idea that it will be a whirlwind ride. That by the end of this year I will be living with Wendy, my love, and her children. That I will be making friends with her friends and getting to know her parents and doing new things with my life, seeing myself and everything else in new ways.

It is like everything is always starting over and over again.

Sometimes I want to hide beneath the sheets and sometimes I want to run along the beach and stare way, way up at the high, high clouds.

AN INTRODUCTION TO FINISH WITH

And now I find that I am nearing the end of my story. My story has, as all stories do, beginnings and endings even when we do not acknowledge them. All stories are saying something, even when we are unsure what.

What have I been telling you? Shaking my finger and saying?

'Listen here, I have something to say!'

I have been telling you something of my life, only something. It is only a couple of years ago that I wrote a book about my life that was completely different, a book about the sea and mountains and childhood and forests and beaches.

This one, well, you know. You have read it. Unless you are like Wendy and read the last page first.

I think this story, and it is a story, because nothing is ever really real – or maybe everything is – is about trying to understand my diagnosis because so many books are written about people like me and not by people like me.

It is about talking about what it is like to be detained, because few of us have that platform.

It is about how marriages can destroy people even when they are wonderful and how abuse can be a mutual thing. It is about how the absence of your child can obliterate you and it is about how my life is more than a marriage, more than partnership and fatherhood and more than work; more than all the labels you and I apply to each other.

And it is a love story.

I don't know whether it is a love story that says that love and cuddles stop that loneliness and isolation.

Just a wee while ago, a tiny wee bit ago, I could not even glimpse the thought that I might be with someone again, that I might want to share my life and my dreams. I bought everything for one person, planned everything I did and wanted for a life apart. But somehow that bleakness and that place where I did not really care what happened to me, what my future was, has gone and been replaced by the dream and the reality and the risk of love.

But it hasn't really gone, because I know that no one thing takes away that bleakness; because too many people like me watch rom coms with smiles on our faces, dreaming away, only to wake to the mess of a partnership gone wrong, the humiliation of relationships starting and stopping. The indignity of placing our heart with other people before we have even cleaned it up a bit, done some basic maintenance on it.

My story is a way of challenging me and people like me who, in the name of ideology, make out that mental illness has quick obvious solutions if only people were to listen to us. It is a way of saying there is something horrendous about what we experience and that sometimes when we speak up, we do it purely for the relief and liberation of saying, 'This is how it is.'

This is what happens.

Just saying that. Not changing the world except through the astonishing dignity I see in my friends when they talk with openness and honesty, knowing that openness will cause them suffering and also knowing that it will create whole realms of rainbows stretching out of the night.

Lastly, it is my own journey and my own realisation that has grown more and more. The realisation that I, not Graham the Schizophrenic or Graham the Father, Husband, Friend, Worker, but me, who is some combination of all of these, I have been surrounded by loving tender people for much of my life and despite their love and sometimes because of real or imagined resentments, have not allowed myself to understand what I have done to those around me.

It is my offer to those who know me, my offer to say, 'I have been blind and frightened and now, whoever you are, I offer some of what I see of me and you.'

I have not let you know what Wendy is like or told you much about her, but I have included stories and bits and bobs about the last year with her. That is the real story.

This book is called START, because now that my life is beginning to wind down to its finish, I find I am starting again. That I am just about to step out of adolescence into adulthood. An adulthood where I will learn to be as silly as possible. Where, at least in secret, I will dance and where I will also start the stuff I didn't know I could do.

I will listen and hold and try to understand when my love is sad. I will find things to do that bring a smile to people's faces. I will learn to be organised. I will learn to make decisions. I will be responsible and I will be the opposite of responsible.

I will dare to have opinions and I will know that nearly all opinions and values change by and by, and I will learn what Wendy has taught me. That if I stamp my foot for a principle, put everything at stake for a belief, then I will almost certainly have got it wrong.

That my new love story will be learning that changing the world is always suspect even though it consumes so many of us, but making someone you love laugh, or snuggle up to you happily is of value. Helping someone believe in themselves a wee bit more. Cooking a meal, babysitting, walking hand in hand and seeing something bright in the dusk is so much more fun and so much more rewarding than telling everyone how awful everything is.

EPILOGUE ABOUT THAT THING CALLED HAPPINESS

And finally, finally, I have started.

The New Year is here. Next week I go back to work.

In the next two weeks I will almost certainly be sectioned again for another year. Another year of being made to see the people who I know help me and another year of being made to take my injection that I think might help me but don't want to have. Knowing that I will get angry because they have, in so many words, said that as long as I deny I have schizophrenia, as long as I say I don't want to take the medication, I will be made to take it.

Only when I agree with what they say, only when I agree it helps me will they set me free.

Like I said. All the way back to schoolbooks and George Orwell.

And yet I think there is another way of seeing things that is not as black and white as I see them. I think one day I might listen, I might hear. I might draw conclusions and I might move way, way from talking about me and illness and remember sitting on the bench with Wendy in the gathering dusk with a blue sky going black, tinged with red. Cuddled up, watching the crows flying home, probably to the trees beside her house.

And we will smile and I will turn round and I will say:

'Mental illness, so what! I have a life I want to start living. I have a wonderful person to kiss and talk to for a lifetime. I have friends. I have work. I have almost everything I need, if not more. I have everything. I am busy living. I am no villain and no victim. I am neither tragedy nor inspiration. I am Graham, busy learning to be me.'

GOOD MORNING

Lying in our bed, reading a book and listening to the rain falling on the window, leaving slight glimpses of a gleam on the black window above us.

I cannot really understand this feeling. To have someone rest their head on my chest, to feel their breath on me, the occasional twitch of their legs while every so often I will slip onto a new page. Trying to keep the noise to the minimum.

Putting my book down, there is not a sound from the crows that live in the woods outside. Just occasionally, the wonderful noise of the whistle the train makes as it approaches the station. Letting my eyes droop, dropping into a slow doze, catching in the distance the sound of my far off snoring.

Waking. Not believing my love can be thanking me for lying beside her while she slept. Just thinking, *Can this really be happening? A long lazy Saturday.*

A long lazy Saturday doing things I don't do. Sleeping so late, making love, breakfast in bed. A shower and hours sat talking and watching old pop videos on the television.

A lunch of plum tomatoes, mozzarella, avocado, beetroot, homemade bread and homemade bramble vinegar.

Thinking I could so get used to being loved. I could so get used to each of us vying to please each other in a hundred different ways. I could so get used to this life, this delicate destiny neither of us quite believes is happening to us.

Looking back at my poem,

'Wendy will you be mine?'

And thinking,

'I know we cannot be someone else's, but still I'll be yours if you will be mine. And no, I know it's not a contract, and and and...'

And saying to myself,

'I have found the chance to be silly again and trusting again and filled with the shiny, giggling hope of a new future.'

I have found the chance for the joy of something wonderful. I suppose that someone somewhere will read this and you won't know me or have any knowledge of me. I will just be some person, some person speaking away to you from the page.

I need to finish my story. I need to draw this wee stage of my life to a close. Although, as I have said, there is only a start and a close to stories like this when we choose to make it so.

My section. Well, my section expired two days ago. Normally there would be a panic to get me to a tribunal, to get the paperwork done, all the forms completed. But no, in the manner of a story like this, there is a big backlog of people waiting for tribunals, waiting to be listened to, to be heard, to have their rights preserved and their rights protected and their detention discussed and discussed and probably confirmed. And because there is a backlog, I am in a queue. Waiting.

At some undisclosed point in the future I will be informed that there will be a tribunal convened for me. To decide on my section and whether I need to be on one, even though it has already expired.

Actually, my psychiatrist and MHO already agree I need to be on one so I expect it will just be a formality when it does happen.

At the beginning I mentioned weight and fitness and dying early. Well, I had my yearly MOT. My blood sugar is up and remains up. So now I have to phone the action team and presumably they will tell me I now have diabetes and they will start instructing me how to change my life to cope with it.

That's how it goes.

Stories wind along and even when they reach the sea they can form fast currents or rise into the air and become clouds.

My story is winding along. I'm a wee bit bewildered but definitely happy, definitely thinking this world is sometimes brighter than I thought it was.

Wendy's upstairs sleeping. But I think she may be waking soon. I've made coffee for her.

AND WHAT HAPPENED NEXT?

Well, people always do want to have that sense of completion to a story. My story is my life and I do hope that one day I can tell people more about it... But for the moment... What happened? Wendy. My section. My family. My friends. All that stuff?

I was sectioned again. Wendy and I went to the tribunal which was quick and clean and unexpectedly emotional after we left it. In fact, as I write, six years have passed since the last page you read and I am in my tenth year of being held on a compulsory community treatment order. I feel no more clear about it than I used to. Maybe it keeps me alive. I think it probably does. Should I be alive? I am unsure. I am delighted with my new life but sometimes feel so terribly guilty that I have inflicted my presence on Wendy and the wee ones.

So of course that means I left Nairn. I now live in Cardross in the house across from the 'forest'. The little ones spend half their time with us and half their time with their dad, who lives just a hundred yards away down the forest path. They are absolutely wonderful. They just seem to spend their entire life bouncing. Just like puppies, chasing around and then suddenly collapsing in heaps on the ground. I cannot describe how they make me feel but when they greet me with a hug or ask where I am when I am away working, I feel more lucky than I could ever have imagined I would ever feel again.

I now have a ready-made family and a new set of friends. I think I crave things like that. My childhood was a succession of different schools and homes, a series of dislocations with no connections with the past. To be with Wendy, who is rooted in her family and her community, who has spent most of her life living within twenty miles of her birthplace, who is still in touch with her childhood friends; that astonishes me and makes me too feel wonderfully connected, wonderfully secure.

I have not seen my wife and have heard from her only to try to arrange our divorce which I would dearly like to have been done and dusted long before now. I do not hear from my son and do not know where he lives or what he does or how he is. I know he is bound to be someone I would be proud to know and I am proud that I was a part of his growing up. If ever I see him again I will be delighted. It is a lovely dream but for the moment it is just that, a dream of what might happen.

However, I have made contact with three of my wife's sisters: one of my nieces contacted me on facebook and then some others. Then, when my wife's mother was dying, my wife's sisters contacted me so that I could write to her and they let me know that she bore me no ill will. My letter never did get read to her but I am soft with the news that she did not feel as badly about me as I feared. In fact, held me affectionately in her memories. Since their mother died, those three sisters have become estranged from my wife and her other sister. It is sad how such things happen but lucky for us as they come to visit us and we visit them: grown up children, two wee sets of young twins gambolling, meals and barbecues together. Meeting up for coffees, even reinstating the tradition of passing on to me one of my, soon-to-be ex-brother-in-law's old clothes. It astonishes me that my sisters-in-law and their children want to see me. It delights me.

I have a new job. I work for the Mental Welfare Commission for Scotland, involving people in its work. It is a lovely job but part time so I earn much less than I used to. I travel across the country and have got used to the three and half hour round trip to work. I go into secure hospitals and meet people who my heart beats for. People who have got involved in the terrible parts of life, that have caused untold suffering to others and to themselves. I meet people in cafes and garden centres. I visit hospital wards and peer at patients' notes. I meet people with dementia and people with personality disorder, autism, learning disabilities as well as mental illness. And I give speeches.

Last year I spoke in Geneva with the Association for the Prevention of Torture to people from about 13 different countries and this winter I will be speaking to the United Nations Committee against Torture. I spend much of my time feeling nervous about how to express opinions and how to combine them and take account of the views of those who have completely different perspectives to mine.

I think, although I don't work directly for the government, that I am now almost a civil servant! I have a pass on a lanyard to get into the office. I have a laptop which, if I use it at home, I need five different passwords to log in to the internet; all very baffling. I still work for HUG in the Highlands, just for two days a month, as their special advisor and occasionally I do odd bits of work for other organisations.

I have left my friends in the Highlands but many of them keep in touch. I often stay with them when I go back up there to work. I am not that good at keeping in touch but I am learning the importance of it and the wonder of knowing that these new friends I have made since leaving my wife still want to see me.

That is, all except one. Sarah, who was my bedrock for so long, got into a dispute at work which I could not protect her from. Maybe I should never have protected her from such things in the first place. The last six months in Highland were therefore difficult. She stopped all contact with me, blocked me on her phone and Facebook. And her children, especially Cara, who I had babysat every week and been around for, for all of her life, vanished from my life. I found it incredibly painful. Sometimes I wonder if it was my fault, sometimes I think maybe growing up involves losing people precious to you and sometimes I am just plain bewildered.

I have made friends down here; renewing contact with some old friends I left behind when I moved to the Highlands twenty years ago. I have met some amazing new people from work. I am getting to know Wendy's friends and getting to know how to smile at people at the school gate. Every two weeks we visit two friends who live in a sort of castle on the other side of the village. We sit at the table and drink gin and wine. They now put wee things to fiddle with at the seat I sit at, so that I can keep occupied when I am being quiet. We leave around midnight, stagger down the lane, our thin torch beams lighting up the trees and the shadows. It feels pretty good.

My family: my mum and dad, my sister and brother and their families. I am overjoyed that I can now genuinely say that I love them all very much, that I always look forward to the moments we speak on the phone or meet up. Ah, now that is very special. I no longer need to blame, I no longer need some sense of victimhood to shore up my identity. What a change! No longer looking for answers or solutions or baddies to challenge. It makes a huge difference.

And I am still quiet. Wendy says that all her previous partners were quiet but that I excel at it. She has taken to calling me 'the silent man' and sometimes begs me to tell her a story, anything. And sometimes I manage but often I am empty and have nothing to say.

That is the next stage of my adventures. From someone who has sailed the high seas and wandered in different countries, travelled in the hills, to someone who became a slightly rigid socialist intent on changing the world, I am now changing again. I have now learnt to cook with *Frylight* most of the time to suit Wendy's diet. I have taken to visiting theme parks like Disneyland and enjoy every moment of it. I trawl the seashore for seaglass on weekends. I paint walls and plant plants. I watch television first thing in the morning. I have even watched Jeremy Kyle and quite like Judge Rinder. And it is all good. I have no problem with Wendy's daughter believing in fairies and wanting to be a princess and I have no problem with her son being a football fanatic and obsessed with Minecraft on his mum's phone. It is wonderful not having to watch every thought or aspect of living or upbringing for hints of sexism, racism, ageism, disableism, mentalism, classism; to avoid this new puritanism and to just concentrate on being as good and as open as I can be to the people around me, generally liking people but learning that I can dislike some people too.

I still have earnest conversations about the environment. I still feel guilty that I am not helping refugees in the way some of my best friends are, but most of all I am learning not to be scared of myself, not to be scared of other people. I am learning not to get drunk and I am learning to dare to do silly dances for the children, to express an opinion to Wendy, to approach this strange and alien world in the expectation that

255

by the time I retire I might finally consider myself to be approaching adulthood.

It's still frightening. I often stand on the platform at Central Station and feel a compulsion to jump under the train. I worry about people watching me on the way to work, but I no longer keep razor blades in the bathroom. And the last time I felt so much more lost and alien and evil and just wished I could run away to the hills and the sea and cease to be, I found I could turn to Wendy and speak of my fears, push them away, choose to know I am evil and yet still love the world I live in and the people around me.

And Wendy, yes, I am guilty of idolising her and putting her on a pedestal. I don't really care. She is so beautiful and so much fun and so good at talking and so amusing. She is so good at avoiding arguments where people have opinions that have assumed an importance they shouldn't have. She is brilliant at talking to strangers even though she says she is shy, and brilliant at thinking of things to do and getting excited by life. She calls me her bear and imitates the grunting noises I make. She hates my burps but we are both delighted that we can now finally burp and fart in each other's company and so have left behind the sore tummies that plagued our early relationship. She is determined to get me fit so that I do lots more living. She is brilliant at dealing with the children and couldn't care less if she prizes love and softness over routine and good behaviour. She has sudden enthusiasms and then forgets about them, so life is always an adventure. She gets good deals for holidays and doesn't worry about how much money we have. She puts up with my constant tidying and washing and cooking and shopping. She is even promising to listen next time I get obsessed with wills and life insurance and all those boring bits that appear to make life safe.

I am so lucky. I wish all those people I meet through my work, all those people with a mental illness who are my dear friends, had as bright a life as me, were as lucky as me. I even like my new CPN who is young, fun, always positive, always warm, just great for someone like me. I have even been persuaded to apply for disability benefits and got them. So many of the people I know have nothing approaching that. I have love, friends, family, purpose, things to do and things to look forward to. Joy, support when I need it and even when I don't need it and I have money, or at least a little money.

Many people have nothing like that. I would like that to change.

Glossary

Advance Statement: A record of a person's wishes and preferences for their mental health care while they are ill.

Compulsory Community Treatment Order: A compulsory treatment order authorises the detention in hospital and/or treatment of a person in the community for a period of six months initially and then for one year at a time.

Constant obs: This category of observation is used for all patients who present an immediate risk to the health and safety of themselves or others and require a one-to-one nurse patient ration. The patient should not be granted leave.

CPA meeting: The Care Programme Approach (CPA) is a way that services are assessed, planned, co-ordinated and reviewed for someone with mental health problems or a range of related complex needs.

CPN: A registered nurse who works in the community as part of a team, seeing patients with mental health needs, in various settings.

Depot injection: Long-acting depot injections are used for maintenance therapy, especially when compliance with oral treatment is unreliable.

Detained under the Mental Health Act (sectioned): Being 'sectioned' is the term that is often used when someone is detained under the Mental Health Act. The Mental Health Act is the law which can allow someone to be admitted, detained (or kept) and treated in hospital against their wishes.

HUG (action for mental health): An advocacy group speaking for people with a mental illness in Highland.

IPCU (Intensive psychiatric care unit): Provides intensive treatment and interventions to patients who present an increased level of clinical risk and require an increased level of observation.

MHO: A social worker who has special training and experience in working with people who have a mental illness, learning disability or related condition.

Named person: If a person being cared about becomes unwell, they may need to be detained in hospital under the Mental Health Act, or 'sectioned'. If this happens, they can nominate a 'named person', who will look out for their interests.

Occupational therapy O.T.: Provides support to people whose health prevents them doing the activities that matter to them.

Psychiatrist: A physician who specializes in the prevention, diagnosis, and treatment of mental illness.

Psychologist: A mental health professional with highly specialized training in the diagnosis and psychological treatment of mental, behavioural and emotional illness.

'Specialling': Patients at the highest levels of risk of harming themselves or others may need to be nursed within arms length and more than one nurse may be necessary.

Tribunal: An independent organisation set up to make decisions on the compulsory care and treatment of people with mental disorders in Scotland.

Wrap plan: The Wellness Recovery Action Plan (WRAP®) is a personalized wellness and recovery system born out of and rooted in the principle of self-determination.

Abilify: Used to treat the symptoms of psychotic conditions such as schizophrenia and bipolar I disorder (manic depression).

Chlorpromazine/Largactil: Used chiefly as a tranquilizer especially in the form of its hydrochloride to control the symptoms of psychotic disorders (such as schizophrenia).

Depixol and Fluanxol: A typical antipsychotic drug of the thioxanthene class.

Diazepam: A tranquillizing muscle-relaxant drug used chiefly to relieve anxiety.

Fluoxetine: A drug that functions as an SSRI and is administered in the form of its hydrochloride specially to treat depression, panic disorder, and obsessive-compulsive disorder.

Haloperidol: A tranquilizer used especially in the treatment of psychotic disorders, including schizophrenia.

Lorazepam: Used chiefly in the management of acute anxiety and for insomnia.

Olanzapine/Zyprexa: Used to treat the symptoms of psychotic conditions such as schizophrenia and bipolar disorder.

Resperidal/Risperidone: Sold under the trade name Risperdal among others, is an antipsychotic medication. It is mainly used to treat schizophrenia, bipolar disorder, and irritability in people with autism.

Zoplicone: Belongs to a class of medicines commonly called Z drugs. It works by acting on the way messages are sent in the brain, which help people to sleep. It reduces the time it takes for people to fall asleep and increases the length of time people spend sleeping.